ARTS OF INTOXICATION

The Aim, and the Results.

By Rev. J. T. CRANE, D.D.,

AUTHOR OF "POPULAR AMUSEMENTS," "THE RIGHT WAY," ETC.

Φαρμακον νηπενθες.—Homer.

Intoxicated both,
They swim in mirth, and fancy that they feel
Divinity within them breeding wings,
Wherewith to scorn the earth.—Milton.

NEW YORK:
CARLTON & LANAHAN.
SAN FRANCISCO: E. THOMAS.
CINCINNATI: HITCHCOCK & WALDEN.
1871.

PREFACE.

THE great problem of the times is, "What shall be done to stay the ravages of intoxication?" The evil pervades every grade of civilization as well as all depths of barbarism, the degree of its prevalence in any locality being determined apparently more by the facilities for indulgence than by climate, race, or religion.

In heathen China the opium vice is working death. On the eastern slopes of the Andes the poor remnants of once powerful nations are enslaved by the coca-leaf, and the thorn-apple, and thus are fixed in their fallen estate. In Europe and America the nations who claim to be the leaders of human progress are fearfully addicted to narcotic indulgences, which not only impose crushing burdens upon them, wasting the products of their industry and increasing every element of evil among them, but render even their friendship dangerous to the savage tribes whom their commerce reaches. Italy, France, Germany, England, and the United States are laboring beneath a mountain weight of crime, poverty, suffering, and wrong of every description, and no nation on either continent is fully awake to the perils of the hour. Questions of infinitely less moment create political crises, make wars, and overthrow dynasties.

But the day of total darkness and inaction is past. Especially in England, Scotland, and America, a body of people highly respectable both in numbers and in character are making resistance to this public enemy a specialty of benevolent effort. To aid them is the bounden duty of every patriot, and, above all, of every Christian. Their gigantic foe, like the Philistine, incased from head to foot in armor of brass, rushes to the encounter with sword and glittering spear. They, like the youthful son of Jesse, come only with simple trust in God, and with the shepherd's sling and the smooth stones of the brook, the unpretending weapons of truth and humanity.

The author desires to place this little work as a small pebble in the scrip of the champion of the right, hoping that it has a true mission, and will not fail to hit some head, giant or dwarf, before it falls to earth. He has long felt that a somewhat thoughtful and systematic discussion of the whole subject in a volume of moderate size, giving the latest and clearest verdicts of science without the formalities of scientific method, is needed for the more vigorous prosecution of the reform, and the achievement of more substantial success. This volume is an attempt in that direction. Of its quality the reader must judge.

If there should seem to be in it any departure from old methods of interpreting the phenomena of alcoholic action, the reader will feel that, in view of recent research and discovery, such departure is inevitable. The facts, newer or older, hitherto scattered or seemingly contradictory, refuse to crystallize in any other form. This reconciles, combines them all, and gives each its fitting place. J. T. C.

NEWARK, N. J., *June* 30, 1870.

CHAPTER I.

THE ART OF INTOXICATION NOT A DEVICE OF MODERN TIMES.

CHAPTER II.

MYSTERY AND DISCOVERY.

CHAPTER III.

COCA-LEAF—THORN-APPLE—BETEL-NUT.

CHAPTER IV.

TOBACCO: THE HISTORY.

CHAPTER V.

TOBACCO: THE HABIT.

CHAPTER VIII.

THE OPIUM HABIT.

CHAPTER IX.

ALCOHOL: ITS PRODUCTION.

CHAPTER X.

ALCOHOL: ITS DELUSIONS.

CHAPTER XI.

ALCOHOL: ITS REAL EFFECT.

CHAPTER XII.

ALCOHOL: THE HEREDITARY EFFECT.

CHAPTER XIII.

ALCOHOL: THE WRONG OF INDULGENCE.

CHAPTER XIV.

ALCOHOL: THE FOLLY OF BEGINNING.

CHAPTER XV.

ALCOHOL: THE STRENGTH OF THE ENEMY.

CHAPTER XVI.

ALCOHOL: THE DAMAGE DONE.

CHAPTER XVII.

ALCOHOL: REMEDIAL MEASURES.

THE

ARTS OF INTOXICATION.

CHAPTER I.

THE ART OF INTOXICATION NOT A DEVICE OF MODERN TIMES.

Is there any thing whereof it may be said, See, this is new? it hath been already of old time, which was before us.—ECCLESIASTES.

SOME twenty-eight centuries ago Homer sung his lofty song of heroes and of war. He pictures Ulysses, the wise King of Ithaca, impelled by the solemn compact into which he had entered, bearing himself nobly among the warriors before the walls of Troy, and noted equally for his sagacity and his valor. After a ten years' siege, the city is captured by stratagem, the inconstant Helen is restored to her husband, Menelaus, and the Greek princes set out for home. Ulysses wanders from the way, and for ten years he journeys deviously over land and sea. His subjects lament him as among the lost, and his wife, Penelope, is accounted a widow. Sundry princes come to Ithaca seeking her hand in marriage. She will not believe that her husband is dead. With a confidence that never wavers, she assures her son Telemachus that his loved father will yet return. But the weary years pass on, and no tidings are heard from the absent king. Her suitors become importunate. She finally promises to choose a husband from among them as soon as she shall complete a certain piece of tapestry then in the loom. But what she weaves by day she unravels by night, and the work is never done. When prince or warrior urges his plea, or her people hint that she has worn her widow's weeds long enough, she points to the unfinished web and bids them wait a little longer.

Meanwhile their son, Telemachus, now grown to man's estate, resolves to set forth in search of his father. In his journeyings he comes to Sparta, and becomes the guest of Menelaus and Helen, for whose sake Ulysses left his home long years before. Telemachus does not at once announce his name and parentage, but an allusion which Menelaus makes to the brave and wise Ulysses overcomes him, and he covers his face with his purple robe and weeps.

Telemachus then reveals himself, and is received with great distinction as the son of the Spartan king's noblest friend. A royal banquet is prepared, and the king and his nobles, the stranger prince and his attendants, sit down to the feast. Helen exerts herself to soothe the sorrow of her distinguished guest. With her own fair hands she prepares a *nepenthe*, φαρμακον νήπενθες, a magic draught which has the power to banish grief and pain, and bring peace to the troubled spirit. The poet thus describes it:

Meantime, with genial joy to warm the soul,
Bright Helen mixed a mirth-inspiring bowl,
Tempered with drugs of sovereign use, to assuage
The boiling bosom of tumultuous rage,
To clear the cloudy front of wrinkled care,
And dry the tearful sluices of despair.
Charmed with that potent draught, the exalted mind
All sense of woe delivers to the wind.
Though on the blazing pile his father lay,
Or a loved brother groaned his life away;
Or darling son, oppressed by ruffian force,
Fell breathless at his feet, a mangled corse;
From morn to eve, impassive and serene,
The man, entranced, would view the deathful scene.
These drugs, so friendly to the joys of life,
Bright Helen learned from Thone's imperial wife;
Who swayed the scepter where prolific Nile
With various simples clothes the fattened soil.

Odyssey, Book IV.

During the wanderings of Ulysses an adventure befell certain of his companions, the story of which forms a very appropriate sequel to that of the draught which Helen prepared for Telemachus. According to the ancient fable, Circe, the daughter of Helios, was skilled in magic, and knew charms and drugs by which she could accomplish whatever she chose to undertake, provided the victim of her arts would drink of the cup which she mixed for him. She was married to the Prince of Colchis, but desiring to reign alone, she poisoned her husband. Banished for this crime to a little island on the coast of Italy, she there dwelt in solitary grandeur, the terror of the wise. Ulysses, in his weary wanderings, landed on her dangerous shores, and not knowing her character, chose by lot certain men to visit her palace and solicit her aid. As they drew near the gates a thousand wolves, with lionesses and she-bears, rushed out to meet them. But the savage beasts, instead of tearing them to pieces, began to wag their tails and fawn upon the strangers. Then came a crowd of smiling maidens, who welcomed them with flattering words, and led them into a marble hall. Here they found Circe clothed in robes embroidered with gold, sitting upon a throne of state. Her attendants were not combing the snowy wool, nor nimbly plying the distaff, as was the custom even in the homes of princes in those simple times, but were gathering herbs of various kinds. These the sorceress received from their hands, assorted according to their various powers, and laid aside for future use.

When the Greek warriors approached she received them graciously, and promised all that they asked. She then bade an attendant prepare a cup of wine, milk, honey, and parched barley for her guests, to which she herself added certain juices from the gathered herbs; and as they drank, she stretched forth her wand and gently touched their heads, and, lo! in a moment they began to lose the human form; the hair of their heads became bristles, their faces stretched out into snouts, their hands and feet turned into hoofs, and their voices changed tc a horrid grunt. They were no longer men, but swine. Luckily, one of the Greeks had been wise enough to refuse the poisoned chalice. He fled to the ship, and told of the terrible misfortune which had befallen his comrades. Ulysses hastened to the palace, sword in hand, and demanded the release of his friends. Circe, awed by his bold demeanor, yielded, and reversing her powerful spell, restored them to their original forms. They again were men.

Here, then, are two magic cups, the one proffered in the kindness of primitive hospitality, and working only what was deemed a good result; the other given in treachery, and working only evil effects. How much of historic verity underlies these stories it is not easy to determine. The description of Circe and her malignant deeds may be indicative only of the superstition of the times, the popular belief that magic is a true art, and that those skilled in it wield a fearful power over others by means of charms and incantations.

The account which Homer gives of the *nepenthe* which Helen mingled for Telemachus, on the contrary, appears to contain a vein of genuine truth. It seems to hint that discoveries had been made in regard to the properties of certain plants, by the use of which abnormal states of mind could be produced at will. There is an inclination to accept the story of Homer as based upon fact, and to see in it an intimation that even in that early age men had found out the secret of intoxication, and knew more than one way to produce it. Alcoholic wine and its properties were certainly well known at that time, but the *nepenthe* seems to have contained some ingredient the knowledge of which was treasured up as a rare and valuable secret. What this ingredient was none can tell, and the learned conjecture variously. Some fancy that it was opium, others the hemp poison.

This, however, is of little moment. If we could succeed in disinterring all the buried knowledge of the past, it is not probable that we should add to the list of known intoxicants. The fact that interests us most is, that men thirty centuries ago were acquainted with the dangerous joys of intoxication, and knew how to secure them. They had found a care dispeller, which was able to render the soul insensible to the ills of life, and weave about men a spell so potent, and hold them wrapped in factitious enjoyment so deep and over-mastering, that for the time nothing could avail to rouse them from it, or make them conscious of pain, danger, or sorrow.

Here, therefore, on the classic page stands one of the first intimations which the records of the past give of a perilous practice to which the reckless are tempted to resort when they would lend a wilder pleasure to their revels, and the weak and the despairing when they feel or fear that the battle of life is going against them. The *nepenthe* of Homer is the type of the whole list of substances to which men weakly and wickedly have recourse when they seek either release from the ills that actually press upon them, or crave enjoyment not legitimately within their reach.

The cup which Spartan Helen prepared is described as being potent for both these purposes.

It deadened the sensibilities so that a man would shed no tears even at the funeral of his father, nor would he feel horror or concern if his brother or his son were murdered before his eyes. It could charm away his sorrow without removing in any wise the cause of grief. It could fill with joy when the realities of the hour demanded tears, and when mirth was only a ghastly mockery. The two stories, read together, typify the whole practice and the fruit of the dangerous arts of intoxication, the unnatural devices by the use of which men, for a few fleeting moments, cease to feel the toil, the care, the various disquietudes which belong to this state of trial, and secure an artificial but pleasurable mental frame, which only lacks permanence to make it true insanity. The story of Helen and Telemachus reveals the aim; the fable of Circe and the Greek warriors shows us the result. At the beginning the victim is exalted beyond the reach of earthly ill; at the end he is brutalized and ruined. The whole process is an abuse, a cheat, a folly, a crime.

Yet from the earliest ages men have known how to prepare some form of a *nepenthe.* The Scriptures tell us that Noah planted a vineyard, and on one occasion drank of the wine until he was drunken. Very possibly the process of fermentation had not before been noticed, its results were not known, and the consequences in this case were wholly unexpected. The Hindoo Vedas, which are supposed to be as old as the Hebrew Pentateuch, inform us that in the remotest ages to which they refer, an intoxicating beverage called *soma* was prepared from the fermented juice of a plant, and was so highly esteemed that it was offered to the gods in worship. The people attributed even supernatural powers to the *soma,* regarding it as the vivifying principle of the universe.

The ancient Egyptians made wine of figs, pomegranates, and the sap of the palm. They also made an intoxicating beer from barley.

Sculptures and paintings as old as the Pharaohs represent men carried home by their servants in a state of helpless inebriety, and even women vomiting from the effects of drink.

If, as Homer declares, Helen learned from the Egyptians how to prepare the *nepenthe*, very possibly there was in it and its effects nothing that would pass for a mystery in our day. It is worthy of note, also, that all of the four ingredients of the cup of Circe named by the poet are used and abused by the moderns for purposes of intoxication. The only marvel is, that the sorceress having put into the cup four different substances from which alcohol may be made, should think it necessary to add any thing else.

It is sufficiently clear that the use of intoxicants is no modern invention. Nor are the effects in anywise different. The Hebrew Scriptures, the Hindoo Vedas, the Sculptures of the ancient Egyptians, the poets and historians of Greece and Rome, all tell the same sad story of fascination, enslavement, and ruin.

CHAPTER II.

MYSTERY AND DISCOVERY.

Lo, this only have I found, that God hath made man upright; but they have sought out many inventions.—ECCLESIASTES.

THE union of the soul with the body in which it dwells is an unfathomable mystery. What tie binds them? Iron may be welded to iron, and wood may be mortised to wood. Material substances of diverse properties may be made to adhere to each other. But how shall spirit be welded to matter? How shall the immortal mind, the invisible, intangible soul, which "hath not flesh and bones," be so shut up and fixed in a material body that it must not only stay within the walls of its living prison, but never exercise its powers independently; never act, save by the medium and through the aid of the gross earthly organization, "this muddy vesture of decay?" The dependence is indeed mutual. When the material nature is paralyzed the spirit seems powerless. Separated from the spirit, the body dies, dissolves, turns again to dust. By what golden bond of unity are these two, so dissimilar in their nature, joined in so close a fellowship?

This, however, is but the beginning of mysteries. Not only does one part of our nature seem dependent on its fellow, either for existence or for something to work by, but the one influences the other, modifies all its activities, and colors all its life. How can the mind tire? The muscle is worn down by prolonged labor, because its very substance is thus reduced in weight and volume; the nerve may fail because its powers are exhausted; but how can the immortal spirit be wearied by its own action? Yet rest and sleep are needful to those whose toil seems to be solely that of the mind.

And how shall we explain the decline which marks the approach of age? The mental faculties, as well as the bodily powers, feel the weight of years. The reason ceases to be the sure guide which it once was; the memory no more produces its rich treasures at a moment's warning; the will has no longer the promptness and the force which marked it in the days which are gone. Why all this change? Does mind decay? Do souls grow old? Or is it only the dulling of the tools with which the mind works, the darkening of the windows through which it looks?

And how shall we explain what we call mental disorder? Can the immaterial spirit become diseased, so that it beholds what the eyes do not see, and hears imaginary voices where there is only silence, and lives an ideal life which has no foundation in the real and the true? Something is wrong; but what is wrong? Can the mind itself, the soul, the spirit, be unhinged and disorganized? Or is it only the derangement of the apparatus by which the mind acts?

But there are still more curious effects of this wondrous union of mind and matter. Each can be reached, and not only the amount but the nature of its action changed by means of the other. When a man is weak in body, cold and hungry, he is very apt to be deficient in confidence and courage; he tends to be despondent, and to look at the dark side of things. Give him food and rest and the clouds disperse, or at least grow thinner. Some diseases announce their attacks first by mental depression, and the first token of recovery is seen in the lightening of the shadows. Thus the body affects the mind and colors its vision.

Moreover, the process may be reversed, and the body affected by means of the mind. Break to the mother the sudden news that her child has just been killed in the street, and she utters a piercing cry and falls at your feet as one dead. Why is this? You did no violence to the physical nature. You merely touched with a thought the immortal mind. With a thought, which has no length, or breadth, or weight, you smote the inner spirit, and the outer frame, built up of solid material substance, sinks beneath the invisible blow. Who can explain? We may indeed utter sounding phrases, and give the fact a score of learned names; but this only "darkens counsel by words without knowledge." The working of the same principle is seen and felt in the commonest experiences of daily life. A pathetic story calls forth a tear, or words of commendation a blush. A fancied insult makes the face redden, and the eyes flash with indignation.

And still another thing is worthy of notice. We are susceptible of excitement, a mounting tide of mental, emotional, and physical energy, which rises more or less gradually, and, when at its height, sweeps along with a power to which in our cooler moments we are strangers, and things at other times impossible are done with ease. The soldier, worn down by a long march, is so weary that he can hardly carry his weapons; but when the battle opens, with its exciting sights and sounds, its rapid evolutions, its fierce passions, his once languid frame becomes as steel for strength and endurance. The public speaker begins his address slowly and calmly, but warms as he advances, till his face glows, his voice resounds, his whole being kindles, and his thoughts, like the arrows of old Acestes, flame as they fly.

This is the hour when the man has the full use of all his powers. Roused thus, the student reciting his lesson, the young lady performing on the piano, the carpenter driving his saw, the poet penning an ode, will all do their best. These are the times when the heart beats strongly, the blood flows in full channel, and we are ablest to move others, and are ourselves most easily moved, either to love or anger, merriment or tears.

And there is enjoyment in these tides of power. We love to feel every nerve strung, and every muscle full of bounding blood. We love to watch the flash of our own thoughts, and feel the rising strength of our own emotions, and know that in whatever direction we choose to turn, we are prepared to do and be our best. There is a charm in this waking up of dormant forces, this tuning of the whole instrument to its highest tension. In its better forms, it is one of the sweetest pleasures known to the human mind and heart. The public speaker feels it on the platform, and perhaps unduly prolongs his discourse because he so enjoys the flow of living thought and the rush of winged words that he takes no note of time; nor will the audience complain of the length of the address if they too get fairly afloat on the mental tide which sweeps him away. The editor, the historian, the poet know something of the same joy, and call it their "inspiration."

It must be confessed that, in some of its aspects, mental and emotional excitement is not entirely free from peril. Not only does the intellect work more promptly and powerfully, but the passions in general are more excitable. Where the moral principles are good, and their supremacy is established, these times of exaltation are the golden moments of all holy resolve and lofty action. Where the heart is evil, it is the "hour and the power of darkness," when all crime becomes possible, and the whole being bends before the force of passion and is swept along by the tide of death. If the soul has no settled habits of action, no certain anchorage, it is the day of danger, when reason is less cool and caution is less alert, and watchful and wily tempters of every sort seize the opportunity to play their arts to deceive and destroy.

As this mental exaltation, this emotional glow, brings with it augmented enjoyment, it is natural that we should feel, now and then, the desire to climb the height. But how shall we accomplish it?

There are various methods, some normal and wise, some otherwise. Among minds not beyond a certain degree of development, there is a mechanical way which seems to answer the purpose. Every body has noticed that children engaged in active, noisy play often get into a wild excitement in which they forget every thing else, and give themselves wholly to the reckless merriment of the moment. Mere motion seems to be a sufficient excitant in such cases. We find another illustration of the same thing in the Dervises of the East, who whirl about in giddy circles till they are wrought into a perfect frenzy. Possibly the same principle has something to do with the dances of our fashionable society.

But there is a "more excellent way" than this, one which is higher, nobler, more worthy. It is possible, indeed, to make a man laugh by tickling him with a straw; but it is more respectable to do it with an idea. He that gave our nature its depths did not design that those depths should be stirred by trifles. He gave them not for luxury, but utility in the great aim and work of life. He never intended that the deepest, richest tones of our nature should be evoked by every careless touch of the keys. Human wants, human affections, the demands which belong to time, and the infinite motives which come to us from the eternal world, are all designed to touch each its appropriate spring.

And, without controversy, religion ought to stir our hearts with a deeper, higher, mightier emotion, and hold us under its influence more continuously than all earthly concerns. The tides of divine joy should pour in a broader, fuller stream than every other. The light of every earthly expectation should be as darkness when compared with the radiance of heavenly hope. The exalted enjoyments of devotion should be richer, sweeter to our souls a thousand-fold, than all worldly success or worldly pleasure. And every right affection, every rational hope and desire, is meant to be a motive power, and according to its value, to stir the heart, and breathe into the soul inspirations which lend light to the eyes, make the cheek glow, and send the blood bounding along its channels.

But man has made a fearful Discovery. He has found out, not how to produce these exalted mental states at will, but how to imitate them. He has learned how to counterfeit the golden coin with which God pays the worthy laborer. It has been discovered that certain poisonous drugs, differing in the kind and the degree of their effects, are potent to lay a spell upon soul and body; and, while every mental faculty is unhinged, and every physical power is benumbed, and the whole being rendered helpless and degraded, the abused body may lie steeped in sensuous enjoyment, and the abused mind be cheated with a seeming consciousness of unwonted activity and augmented force and brilliancy.

And men have learned to covet the fleeting, unnatural pleasure. They are ready to buy an hour of it with the price of days of lassitude and gloom, and even of pain, remorse, and death. The old fable tells how Dædalus made wings of feathers and wax for himself and his son, and essayed flight among the stars. Icarus, impelled by an evil ambition, soared too near the sun; the wings melted in the solar beams, and the rash adventurer fell into the sea and was drowned.

Man is willing to resort even to these flimsy artifices, although he is well aware that he rises by trick and falls by inexorable law. For the sake of the hour of fevered dreams he is willing to face the horrors of a return to the realities, which his guilty pleasures have despoiled of honor, peace, and virtue.

CHAPTER III.

COCA-LEAF—THORN-APPLE—BETEL-NUT.

And when the woman saw that the tree was good for food, and that it was pleasant to the eyes, and a tree to be desired to make one wise, she took of the fruit thereof, and did eat.—GENESIS.

MANY different substances are used to drug the mind into forgetfulness of care, toil, and grief, and for a brief space fill it with dreamy happiness and a delusive sense of power. No land is so sterile as not to yield, no savage is so ignorant as not to know, some plant which may be employed to secure artificial mental states. The native Kamtschatkan, far away toward the icy pole, is shut off from the means of indulgence found in more sunny realms. Under the slanting rays of his fleeting summer neither wheat, nor maize, nor barley grows.

But a poisonous fungus, a vile toad-stool, springs from the chilly soil, and produces a drug which benumbs the brain, and wraps the whole being in a bewildering, meaningless rapture.

Nor are the barbarous tribes of our own land destitute of ingredients with which to mingle the cup of temporary madness. Long before European traders brought to these Western shores the evil inventions of civilized nations, the Seminoles of Florida had discovered that a tea made of the leaves of the poison holly *(ilex vomitoria)* will excite men to enthusiasm, or even drive them to frenzy.

The narcotics which, on account of the millions whom they enslave, occupy the chief places in the list of the poisons thus employed, are six in number: the Coca-leaf, the Betel-nut, Tobacco, Hemp, Opium, and Alcohol. These are all more or less intoxicating, and so far are alike; yet their modes of action differ in nature as well as in degree. Some of them lull soul and body into delicious repose, and open the ivory gate of waking dreams. Some spend their force chiefly on the animal part of human nature. Each has a power and tendency of its own. Moreover, under the spell of the same intoxicant, men of different character, mentally and physically, will exhibit corresponding differences in the effect. To trace each peculiar result to its source lies beyond the reach of our nicest investigation, yet the fact is indisputable. We will consider each of these intoxicants more or less briefly, according to the degree of practical interest which attaches to it, and the amount of light which its discussion will shed upon the general subject.

COCA.

Among the Andes of Peru and Bolivia live the remnants of the once powerful race which the Spaniards three hundred and forty years ago found on the western coast of South America. The uncounted millions over whom the Incas swayed the scepter have dwindled down to a comparative few. They are an oppressed and degraded people, superstitious, ignorant, and helpless, whose social position is worse than that of the freedmen of the United States. They constitute the laborers of the countries where they live, toiling at all kinds of hard work in which unskilled mind and muscle find scanty remuneration. They cultivate the soil, dig in the mines, and carry burdens among the narrow passes of the mountains. Poor, despised, with little of heart or hope for nobler pleasures, they find a *nepenthe* in the leaves of a shrub possessing peculiar properties.

The coca-bush grows to the height of six or eight feet, with white flowers and small bright green leaves. It is a native of the eastern slopes of the Andes. It has been cultivated for ages in regular plantations, and thousands of acres of the best land are devoted to it. The leaves when full grown are gathered and dried for use. A coca orchard produces three crops in a season, and the annual yield of an acre varies from five hundred to eight hundred pounds.

Coca is the favorite narcotic of populations numbering several millions, and the annual consumption is estimated at twenty-five or thirty millions of pounds.

There are two or three ways of using the leaf. Sometimes the Indian makes an infusion of it, and drinks the tea. The more common mode is to carry the leaves in a pouch and chew them like tobacco. A little quicklime sprinkled upon the leaf before it is rolled into the quid is supposed to improve the flavor and add to the effect. But the *coquero,* unlike the chewer of tobacco, cannot enjoy his drug unless, for the time being, he devotes himself solely to it. Labor, exertion of any kind, seriously interferes. Therefore three or four times a day the miner lays aside the pick, and the bearer his burden, and the horseman dismounts. Sitting deliberately down, he opens his pouch, and, thoughtfully choosing a sufficient quantity of leaves, touches them with the lime, rolls them up in a ball, and puts them into his mouth. Then, stretching himself out on the grass, he chews the coca, swallows the greenish juice, and is wrapped in silence and a repose which is almost torpor. Nothing can stir him. No matter how valuable the moments, how pressing the emergency, how urgent his master, he will not move. When twenty or thirty minutes have elapsed he starts up, throws away the spent coca-leaves, and declares that he no more feels weary, that his hunger no longer annoys him, and that he is now ready for his toil, or the heavy burden and the mountain path.

The Indians are completely enslaved by the vile habit. They regard the plant as an aid and a solace without which life itself would be a burden. The use of coca is so old that the traditions of the various tribes give no hint of its origin. It had a place even in their heathen religion. The priest burned coca on the altar of his idol, and deemed the smoke an acceptable incense. He thought that if he prayed under the influence of the magic leaf he was surer to be heard. Though the old idolatry has departed, and the Indians are now adherents of the Romish Church, ancient superstitions have not wholly lost their hold. Even now at funerals they fill the mouth of the corpse with coca, to secure for the soul an easy passage to heaven.

The simple fact in the case is, the coca-leaf is a powerful narcotic and intoxicant. The intoxicating principle is indeed peculiar to itself; but while it is unlike other intoxicants in some respects, it agrees with them in all the main features. There is in coca an element which has power to allay nervous irritation, relieve weariness, hunger, and pain, and fill the mind for a brief space with a dreamy sense of happiness. As in the case of other intoxicating substances, the indications of danger at the beginning are such as create little alarm; for awhile the victim thinks that it does him good, and sometimes long periods elapse before the day of reckoning comes.

But what we term moderation is hard to maintain, and excess is ruin. The confirmed victim of coca often loses all self-control, all self-respect, and becomes wretched and degraded beyond description. It is said that the vice fastens on him with an iron grasp, even harder to escape than that of alcohol. His gait becomes unsteady, his skin is yellow, and purple rings encircle his dim and sunken eyes; his breath is foul, his lips perpetually quiver as with fear or despair, his mind is feeble, unhinged, and full of visions which he mistakes for reality. Complicated diseases attack almost every vital organ; the appetite becomes capricious, the digestion impaired; and finally, loathing all healthful food and insanely craving abominable things, he fears to look his fellow-men in the face, he flies from their presence, and in some hiding-place gives himself up without restraint to his vice and succumbs to his fate. The general melancholy which travelers remark in the faces and the demeanor of the populations addicted to the use of coca must be caused in no small degree by the unnatural habit to which, for ages, they have been addicted.

THE THORN-APPLE.

A species of datura *(D. Sanguinea)* is used for purposes of intoxication in some parts both of the old world and the new. One variety of the thorn-apple is a very common plant, a weed with an unsavory smell and unsavory name, which is found growing about piles of old rubbish, with its trumpet-shaped flowers, and the prickly seed pod which gives it the name which it bears. The red thorn-apple is mentioned in connection with coca, because the same Indians who employ the coca-leaf as a solace in toil and trouble use it to secure the wild raptures of a deeper and more rapid inebriety. An intoxicating drink of fearful power is made of the seeds of the datura.

The Indian, weighed down by the miseries of his present condition, tries to alleviate his sorrows by recollections of the past. The traditions of his people tell him of the ages when they were rich and powerful, and the foot of the alien oppressor had never profaned his natal soil. He strives to lighten the gloom of his wretched daily life by reviving the buried glories of his race. While his whole being is under the mastery of the potion the golden age seems to return, and in his delirium he fancies that he beholds the palaces of the Incas, and holds converse with the spirits of departed heroes. A traveler in Peru saw a man under the influence of the apple, and thus describes the effect:

"Shortly after having swallowed the beverage he fell into a heavy stupor. He sat with his eyes vacantly fixed on the ground, his mouth convulsively closed, and his nostrils dilated. In the course of about a quarter of an hour his eyes began to roll, foam issued from his half opened lips, and his whole body was agitated by frightful convulsions. These violent symptoms having subsided, a profound sleep of several hours succeeded. In the evening, when I saw him again, he was relating to a circle of attentive listeners the particulars of his vision, during which he alleged he had held communication with the spirits of his forefathers. He appeared very weak and exhausted."

It is said that in ancient Greece the seeds of the thorn-apple were used by the priests who presided at the shrines of heathen oracles to produce visions and give the semblance of supernatural influence. It is known that in New Granada the priests in the temple of the Sun used it in their deceptions, and the incoherent mutterings which it produces were represented as the voice of the gods.

The plant is an intoxicant of the worst type. Here, at home, the seeds are sometimes eaten by little children, and produce delirium, accompanied by spectral illusions. It is said that in some parts of India robbers use it to stupefy their victim, hovering about the traveler as his food is prepared, and insinuating a pinch of the powdered seed into the vessel, and then waiting for the inevitable results. Every part of the plant possesses narcotic properties, and the dried leaves smoked in a pipe are even dangerously intoxicating.

THE BETEL-NUT

Of India is used as a mild narcotic by about one hundred millions of people. This is the seed of the Areca Palm, a species of tree found in abundance in India, especially along the southern slopes of the Himalayas. It is also cultivated extensively along the eastern coast, and in Ceylon and the adjacent islands. The tree grows to the height of about thirty feet. The nut is about an inch long and of a conical shape. It is prepared for chewing by being cut in pieces, sprinkled with quicklime, and wrapped in the leaf of a pepper plant. The quid thus made up is called a *buyo*, and it is a common custom to prepare for a journey by making a quantity of *buyos* for consumption on the road. The nuts, with lime and leaves, are carried in pocket boxes, like tobacco. The quid loses its virtue after half an hour of mastication; and, where indulgence is not limited by poverty, a fresh supply speedily succeeds the exhausted *buyo*, and the process goes on from morning to night with few and brief intermissions.

The effect of the use of betel has not been thoroughly investigated. The first and most obvious result is to stain the mouth red and create a flow of red saliva. The effect upon the nerves is evidently narcotic. When chewed in considerable quantities it creates giddiness. The habit obtains a very decided hold upon those who use the nut, so that they suffer more from a scanty supply of betel than from short rations of food. The Hindoo seems to rely upon this drug for exhilaration and for solace. He fancies that it does him good in every way, helps him in his toils, lightens the weariness of a journey, and yields him comfort in the hour of anxiety or sorrow. The aggregate consumption of betel among the various populations of Asia is estimated at two hundred thousand tons or more annually.

CHAPTER IV.

TOBACCO: THE HISTORY.

A good vomit, I confess; a virtuous herb if it be well qualified, opportunely taken, and medicinally used; but, as it is commonly used by most men, which take it as tinkers do ale, 'tis a plague, a mischief, a violent purger of goods, lands, health; hellish, devilish, and damned tobacco; the ruin and overthrow of body and soul.—*Burton's Anatomy of Melancholy.*

WHEN Columbus landed on the island of Hispaniola, and sent out parties of explorers to discover all that they could concerning the strange new world, his scouts reported, on their return to the ship, that they had met with some of the natives, and had seen among them a very singular practice. These savages carried tubes, in one end of which they placed the dry leaves of a plant unknown to Europeans, and, setting fire to it, blew the smoke out through their mouths and nostrils. Thus civilized man received the first hint of a custom which has since become more widely diffused than any other artificial habit to which men are given.

The source from which the practice was derived is not particularly creditable or promising. Our tobacco habits are borrowed from savages. It is pleasing to observe how faithfully their heathen origin is commemorated in the hideous wooden statuary of the tobacco shops. A half-naked Indian, a negro with distorted face and spasmodic gesture, or some other abominable monstrosity, is deemed the fitting exponent of the whole business.

Tobacco was introduced into Europe by Hernandez de Toledo, who carried it to Spain in the year 1559. The name of the plant is thought by some to be derived from Tobasco, the province of Mexico from which it was imported. Others derive it from Tobago, an island in the Caribbean Sea; others still from *tabac*, the name of the native pipe used in smoking. In the year 1587 a party of colonists whom Sir Walter Raleigh had sent to Virginia returned home to report the failure of the project, but bringing with them to England two new plants, tobacco and the potato. Sir Walter, learning the Indian method of use, procured a pipe, and, experimenting with the strange weed, acquired a love of it. For a time, however, he deemed it prudent to keep his new indulgence a secret. But one day, as the story is told, a servant who had been sent for a mug of beer returned sooner than he had been expected, and found his master in the midst of his performances. Seeing the smoke pouring from Raleigh's mouth and nose, and the whole room filled with the cloud, the terrified servant dashed the beer in his master's face and ran out of the house shouting for help, declaring that Master was on fire inside and burning up.

About the same time, tobacco was introduced into France, Spain, and Italy, not merely as the strange production of lands hitherto unknown, but as a plant of mysterious virtues and great value. The first impression was that it possessed wonderful power as a remedy for disease, and that it was capable of curing almost any of the ills to which flesh is heir. For years the quantity imported was very small, and the price so high that only the rich could afford to use it even as a medicine.

But soon it was discovered that tobacco had other charms than those which pertain to medical matters, and that the use of it was becoming a luxury, and threatening to become a vice. Sober, thinking men were alarmed, not knowing to what dimensions the new indulgence might grow, or what evils might result from it. Certain ill results were not long in showing themselves. Not a few of those who were experimenting with tobacco were infatuated with it, and spent fabulous sums of money in purchasing the means of narcotic enjoyment. The various governments of Europe deemed it a duty to resist this rushing tide of extravagance and folly. James the First, King of England, laid a heavy tax upon the tobacco imported from the Spanish American Colonies ; and, a few years later, tried by law to restrict the cultivation of it in the colony of Virginia.

Not content with the legal method of warfare, James wrote a book against tobacco, entitling his work a "Counterblaste," and denouncing the use of the plant as a practice "loathsome to the eye, hateful to the nose, harmful to the brain, dangerous to the lungs, and in the black, stinking fume thereof nearest resembling the horrible Stygian smoke of the pit which is bottomless."

Other sovereigns joined in the contest against the common enemy, each in a characteristic way. In 1624, Pope Urban forbade the use of snuff in churches. The Russian government prohibited the smoking of tobacco on pain of having the nose cut off by the public hangman. Amurath, the Sultan of Turkey, even made the use of tobacco punishable with death. But books, laws, and taxes, the bulls of Popes, and the edicts of sovereigns, were in vain. The weed which had made its advent in Europe as a remedial agent of marvelous efficacy, had ceased to be regarded as a medicine, but was rapidly assuming the proportions of a luxury, fashionable among the wealthy, and coveted among the poorer classes, who could not afford to indulge in it.

Soon the various governments made the interesting discovery that the popular infatuation could be turned to good account. Kings are always in want of money. Direct taxes are apt to be unpopular. Finding that a heavy impost on tobacco was paid without complaint, the royal authorities soon learned to wink at the growing habits which poured a golden stream into the treasury. At the present hour, the income derived from taxes on tobacco forms so important a part of national revenue that no European government could afford to lose it. The aggregate amount of tobacco annually raised and consumed in all the world was estimated, ten years ago, at one thousand millions of pounds, or five hundred thousand tons. Of this quantity, Asia is credited with 200;000 tons; Europe, 142,000; and America, including the West Indies, 125,000. In 1859, England received $27,000,000, and France $35,000,000, as revenue derived from tobacco. The crop of the United States in 1869 is estimated at two hundred thousand tons, valued, in its raw state, at $40,000,000. The internal revenue tax on tobacco yielded about $30,000,000 in 1869.

Some authorities argue that tobacco is not a plant found first in America and spreading thence through all the world, but that a species of it was known in India and China before the Western Continent was discovered. Wherever it originated, tobacco has circumnavigated the globe, traversing every continent, touching at every island, and planting on every shore the standard of a conqueror. At this moment it sways its scepter over a mightier empire than Alexander or Napoleon ever saw in his rosiest dreams. And it has every-where been a tyrant, and ruled its subjects with a rod of iron, taxing their purse, their time, their health, their usefulness, their happiness, every fiber of the body, and every power of the soul.

And what is tobacco? To the eye it resembles a half grown sunflower plant, differing chiefly in regard to the blossom, which is blue in color and small in size. Every part of the plant contains a peculiar principle, small in quantity but of fearful power, to which the well-known odor, taste, and effect of tobacco are due. Steep the leaves in water to which a little sulphuric acid has been added, and distill the infusion, and there will result a small percentage of volatile oil to which the name of *nicotine* has been given, in honor of Jean Nicot, who introduced tobacco into France. A pound of the dry leaves will yield about an ounce of this substance. In the process of burning, also, tobacco yields this peculiar element in concentrated form.

In regard to the nature of this oil, however obtained, there is but one opinion among chemists and medical authors. In the "*Materia Medica*" of Drs. Wood and Bache it is thus described:

"In its action on the animal system it is one of the most virulent poisons known. A drop of it in a state of concentrated solution was found sufficient to destroy a dog; and small birds perished at the approach of a tube containing it."

These authors add that even when employed as a medicine tobacco should be used with great caution, as it has in several instances caused the death of the patient. One case is described. For some affection of the skin, the head of a child eight years old was bathed with the juice pressed from tobacco leaves, and the helpless innocent died from the effect of the poison. A single leaf moistened and bound upon the chest of a person unaccustomed to the use of tobacco produces the most distressing nausea and vomiting. A single drop of the volatile oil will so poison the air of a whole room that it is almost impossible to breathe in it. Before they learned from the civilized races the use of fire-arms, certain of our Indian tribes were accustomed to poison their war arrows with the oil of tobacco; and those wounded by them became at once sick and faint, and sometimes went into convulsions and died.

There is, we repeat, no difference of opinion among chemists, physiologists, and physicians in regard to the exceedingly poisonous nature of the essential element of the plant. They all hold it to be a deadly venom. Nor does the chemist by his skill create from tobacco a poison which is inert and harmless in the ordinary use. His art merely concentrates, unchanged, that which before existed in the leaf. Remove this essential oil by distillation, and the residue is no longer *tobacco.* The poison is the active principle, to which is due the effect on smoker, chewer, or snuffer. Without the poisonous principle, tobacco would have no power to soothe, fascinate, or enslave.

CHAPTER V.

TOBACCO: THE HABIT.

Stinkingest of the stinking kind,
Filth of the mouth, and fog of the mind.
Africa, that brags her foyson,
Breeds no such prodigious poison.
Henbane, nightshade, both together,
Hemlock, aconite:
Nay rather,
Plant divine, of rarest virtue,
Blisters on the tongue would hurt you!

Charles Lamb's Farewell to Tobacco.

AT the outset of this part of the discussion candor compels me to confess that I have been disappointed somewhat in the result of my investigations. Having no experience of my own to guide me, I have been of necessity dependent on others; and those to whom I have applied for information have manifested a strange inability to give it as fully and clearly as the importance of the subject renders desirable. Why do men smoke or chew? This is a very simple question. When a man takes up his pipe or lights his cigar he is aiming at something. He may never have put the thought into words; still there is a thought which words might express. What, then, does he really propose to himself? Is he seeking merely to escape the uneasiness caused by a few hours' abstinence? Does he look for a subtile, sensuous enjoyment? Or is the effect sought a new mental state? To these plain questions it seems impossible to obtain an intelligible reply from those who certainly ought to know. Replies, such as they are, may not indeed be refused. Some say they smoke "because they like it," or "because it is a habit which they acquired long ago;" but these answers leave the darkness as dense as ever. What, then, is the nature of the effect which tobacco produces upon the mind and body, and from which arises its power to please and to enslave?

The experience of the novice is not hard to comprehend. In ordinary cases it amounts to about this: a very few puffs of the cigar create a tremor of the nerves, a giddiness of the brain, which shows that an enemy is at work. As the smoking proceeds the symptoms grow more decided, the physical distress more apparent, and soon the daring experimenter is, as he thinks, almost dying. His face is livid, like that of a corpse, the breathing is labored, cold drops of sweat stand upon the forehead, the muscles of the whole frame are relaxed and powerless; and the victim of his own folly, or of some one else's cruel sport, pants in an agony of nausea and loathing indescribable. After the lapse of an hour or two the effect subsides, and the smoker revives, and laughs, in a dubious, sickly way, at results which God designed to make a warning so plain that even a fool may not err in regard to its meaning.

But take the case of the confirmed smoker, who has been for years cultivating the habit, and who now consumes daily a dozen cigars. Suppose him to come home at night, after a busy afternoon, during which he has found no time to eat, rest, or smoke. He is weary and hungry; but the strongest, most clamorous appetite is the hunger for tobacco. He therefore eats his supper in haste, that he may smoke at his leisure afterward. His hurried meal being over he seizes his cigar, and the first three whiffs give him more apparent pleasure than all the healthful food, or even luxuries, of which he has partaken. As he puffs away his enjoyment seems to increase. The powerful narcotic begins to operate; his nerves sink into a delicious quiet, and his whole being yields to a pleasant repose. His weariness is at an end; his cares no longer perplex him; the annoyances of the day are forgotten. Lighting a second cigar at the stump of the first, he slides down lower in his chair, gets his feet a little higher, and feels the tide of pleasure still rising. He is conscious of a high state of enjoyment which does not connect itself with any thought, yet seems too ethereal to belong to the body alone. The brain, too, responds to the power of the drug, and he appears to himself to possess unusual clearness and fertility of ideas, and unwonted power of expression. In fact, the man is under the influence of one of the milder forms of intoxication.

And this gentle inebriation is the precise thing for which those hunger and thirst who are the victims of the habit, and the intoxicating element in tobacco is the deadly poison already described. Without the power to intoxicate, tobacco would cease to be what it is. The appetite is not satisfied till enough of the venom has been absorbed to produce a certain effect. The smoker talks of his moderation, his wise caution in the use of his drug. He may explain that he abhors excess, that he chooses the milder sorts of tobacco, and then smokes it, not in the form of a cigar, nor in the short black pipe which conveys to the mouth the full strength of the leaf, but in the new long clay pipe which absorbs much of the essential oil, and precludes injury. O yes; certainly; of course; moderation is necessary.

All this is mere pretense, a self-deception. If a man who is thoroughly committed to tobacco habits uses mild tobacco he uses more of it. If he uses the fresh long clay pipe he will smoke the longer. He will not be content until the brain and nerves are affected to a certain definite degree, and anything short of this is only an aggravation.

I do not think that all are equally susceptible of narcotic influence. Novices, trying their first cigar, are not all affected in the same degree, nor in the same way. In some, nausea will be the strongest symptom; in others, intoxication. Some will make successive trials with little diminution of the woes that attend beginners; others seem to be fascinated almost at once. Before one has learned to tolerate the use, another is already joined to his idol. I have a suspicion, too, that to live among smokers, to inhale constantly the strong fumes of tobacco, produces in some cases not only a degree of physical preparation for the use of it, but tends to implant the appetite, and urge with more or less force in the direction of indulgence. The one whose nervous system responds most promptly and fully to the intoxication will soonest be entangled in the meshes of the habit. Those who get the most enjoyment out of the weed are those upon whose bodies and souls it is liable to set the deepest, broadest mark.

Few devotees of tobacco have an idea of the power of the drug, or how heavy is the hand which it lays upon them, how far it goes into the depths of their being. The Chicago Medical Journal of 1867 describes certain experiments tried with whisky. Four ounces of it were administered to a man, and in half an hour the dose was repeated; in thirty minutes more his pulse was tested, and it was found that within the hour it had risen from 83 to 89, an increase of six pulsations to the minute. This shows the power of alcohol. But the writer once tested the pulse of a clerical friend sitting quietly in his parlor puffing a cigar, and found that in the space of a quarter of an hour the pulsations had increased from 74 to 86 in the minute. In the case of another clerical friend, smoking a pipe in a moderate way, the pulse rose from 70 to 85 within thirty minutes. In neither case, so far as I could see, was there anything but the narcotic to cause acceleration. In both cases, also, the pulse fell off in force, while it increased in frequency.

There are other indications of the power with which tobacco seizes its prey. Especially in the case of the smoker, it tends to deaden soul and body, lessening his inclination and his capacity for exertion of any kind. A man with a cigar in his mouth, and fully under its influence, is slower in thought, slower in action, has fewer ideas, has less feeling, is less of a man in every respect, than at other times. His drug dulls and belittles him at every point. He may not be conscious of his loss. He may aver stoutly that his mind never works with more freedom and force than when he thus indulges. But impartial observers, not addicted to the habit, know better. Note the progress of things at some little gathering of friends for an evening's entertainment. Before supper, and at the table, how animated the conversation, how full of mind, wit, humor, intelligence, force. There is a steady rise in the interest and the mental enjoyment, till the time comes when the host, knowing the habits of his guests, deems it polite to invite them to another room and offer them cigars. From that moment everything declines; the mental interest and pleasure die out, the company tend to be silent, or utter speech which is no improvement on silence, and the affair is over.

I confess that when I penned the preceding paragraph it was not without some hesitation that I set down in plain terms the conclusions to which I had come. Since then, however, I have lit upon the following passage in a recent publication:

"I remember hearing the celebrated M. Bautain, in one of his lectures at the Sorbonne, lament the decline in France of the art of conversation. *Bon vivant* that he appeared in his abundant physique, it was almost whimsical to hear him attribute the misfortune to after dinner smoking. He thought that the post-prandial cigar, banishing men from the influence supposed to rain from ladies' eyes at jousts of wit as well as of arms, and *enveloping them in a haze of oblivious torpor*, had chilled the genial current of that conversational enthusiasm which once made the table-talk of Frenchmen the admiration of cultivated Europe."—Wilkinson's *Dance of Modern Society*.

CHAPTER VI.

TOBACCO: THE QUESTION.

This very night I am going to leave off tobacco. Surely in another world this unconquerable purpose will be realized.—*Charles Lamb's Letters.*

BUT even if we admit that the term intoxication describes properly the effects of tobacco, what harm is there in the indulgence? The intoxication is comparatively slight. It is free from the degradation and the criminal tendencies which mark the grosser forms. It is the handmaid of peace and quiet, of silence and meditation. Tobacco is no shedder of blood, no instigator of noise, strife, and riot. It does not predispose to angry passions, nor to violence of any description. It seems to be the mildest, least harmful phase of the drugging habit; why, then, make war upon it? What if the satisfactions which it bestows be unreal, dreamy; if they be innocent also, why condemn? If men are deprived of this gentle inebriety, will they not rush into something worse?

This is a question worthy of consideration. Nothing is gained by a blind attack on the habits of a people. Even the follies of the age will stand secure, if another folly alone furnishes weapons and leads the campaign against them. I believe the common use of tobacco to be a great evil; but I ask no one to agree with me, except so far as substantial facts, rightly interpreted and candidly weighed, furnish a solid basis of judgment.

1. The use of tobacco is wholly artificial, without foundation in natural wants.

There are easy-going theorizers who never trouble themselves about what ought to be, but delight to find traces of wondrous wisdom in every human weakness, and detect a virtue in every vice. Seeing that the appetite for intoxicants in some form prevails far and wide, these infer that man is impelled to their use by some inherent law of his being, and therefore all that we should attempt is to guide and control the propensity while we gratify it.

This notion is utterly baseless. There is no such natural want, no such physiological necessity. The Roman soldier, without alcohol, tobacco, or even beef, but subsisting on his simple rations of wheat or barley, conquered the world. The Nazarites of ancient Jewish history never tasted even a dried grape, yet the mighty Samson was one of them. The Brahmins of India are really the best class of Hindoos, yet for ages they have abhorred alcohol, and even count themselves defiled if they accidentally inhale the breath of any one who has been drinking the rice brandy of the country. An Arabian family, the sons of Rechab, adopted the principles and practice of total abstinence from alcohol twenty-eight centuries ago, and to-day a powerful tribe claim to be their descendants, maintaining still their wise usages.

And among the nations most given to the use of intoxicants there have always been individuals and classes pure from the vices of their fellows, and certainly not one whit inferior to them in body or mind.

Legitimate argument can be found among the lower grades of animal existence. The human frame is made out of the same material as that of the brute, and is governed by the same general laws. In some points the brute is superior to man. The elephant outlives him a hundred years; the eagle has a keener eye, the lion is stronger, and the antelope swifter. Intoxicants are also within the reach of the brute, but his better instinct warns him, and he obeys. The Indian berry grows in the forest, but the birds do not devour it. The Siberian fungus is found among the mosses upon which the reindeer feed, but they never touch the poisonous thing. The horse, plowing among the corn, bites off the green blades at every chance; but in the tobacco field he will not touch a leaf. No intoxicant is in anywise needful for them. By what law, then, is any intoxicant needful for us? The narcotic indulgences of men are the contrivance of evil ingenuity, a perversion, an abuse, a crime.

2. The devotees of tobacco themselves confess that the habit is useless.

It is not unusual to find men who began to use tobacco with the idea that it would preserve decaying teeth, or with some other notion of the same sort. I never saw one man, however, who, after carefully examining the subject on its own merits, came to the deliberate conclusion that it would be wise for him to learn to use it, and learned accordingly. The great majority declare that they were led into the practice by the example of others, or drifted into it by accident. Not one in a hundred will deny that his habits are an annoyance and a burden to him, and that he often wishes, from the bottom of his heart, that he had never seen the loathsome thing. I never knew a chewer or smoker to advise his children to follow his example. On the contrary, I have known a father, with cruel inconsistency, to punish his sons for not being wiser than he was himself. Looking on from afar, I am willing to accept the testimony of those who ought to know, and to set it down as a certainty, that the habit is not only useless but burdensome.

3. The habit is apt to be unclean and offensive.

Here and there you will find a man who uses the weed in a decent way, so that he gives no offense. In most cases, however, the user of tobacco becomes careless, and forgets that what is so agreeable to him may be offensive to others. The snuffer is as little liable as any to molest his neighbors; but even he may scatter his powder about, while his nasal exercises are anything but harmonious to the ear or pleasant to the eye.

The smoker cannot gratify his desires without poisoning the very air for others to breathe; his clothes, his books, the house in which he lives, every thing that belongs to him becomes tainted, and exhales an ill odor which he does not suspect, but of which others are painfully conscious. This cannot be deemed a trifle, especially in public men. A minister, for instance, piously engaged in visiting the sick, sometimes calls to see a delicate, consumptive member of his church; and as he sits and talks of heaven the very air of the room becomes full of offensive exhalations, which compel the throwing open of doors and windows the moment he leaves the house.

The chewer keeps up an incessant spatter of saliva; nor can he open his mouth without showing that it is "full of all uncleanness." The defilement of the floors in public places and public conveyances will hardly bear an allusion. Such men ought to herd by themselves, and when they travel, ride in the cattle train. Is it wise for any man, especially in professional life, to carry such a weight in the race!

4. Tobacco habits lessen both physical and mental activity.

As has been shown in a former chapter, the effect of tobacco is to increase the frequency of the pulse, while it greatly diminishes the force. Physical energy declines with the declining circulation. The drug affects the brain and nervous system, diminishing the excitability. With the lessening nervous force, there is a diminution of intellectual and emotional activity and vigor. Thus the influence exerted upon the whole man, physical, mental, and emotional, dulls, retards, and diminishes his powers of every kind. He cannot act as quickly, nor think as rapidly, nor feel as strongly. A man smoking a cigar is not master of his real mental forces, nor can he work so well at any craft. If the laborer assures me that if he smokes while at his work he feels less fatigue at the close of the day I believe him, and see a reason for it. A man with a pipe in his mouth will not be likely to work hard enough to hurt him.

Again, a certain amount of active exertion is necessary to every man, and nature demands it. While we rest, the nervous energy accumulates like steam in the engine, and we become uneasy, and feel that we must get about something. But when the impulse is strongest, the devotee of tobacco invokes the paralyzing spell of the drug, and soon the impulse subsides, and the golden hour for high resolve and noble effort is gone. Thus tobacco habits foster indolence, irresolution, and inefficiency.

5. Tobacco habits injure health. Take any one of the facts already given, the fearful power which tobacco exerts over the action of the heart and the circulation of the blood, its effect on the brain and nerves, its power to make soul and body inert and hard to move, and who can resist the conviction that the free use of so potent a drug is unsafe? The individual case may be modified by native strength of constitution, by the degree in which the user is susceptible of the narcotic influence, and by his employ-

ment and general mode of life. A robust man, endowed with little nervous excitability, and engaged in some healthful out-door occupation which has in it little to stir the brain, may be addicted for years to the moderate use and suffer no apparent evil result, especially if he did not acquire the habit until he attained full age. Of those who begin in early boyhood, and on whom the habit really fastens, scarce one escapes serious injury. A French physician, M. Ducaisne, recently investigated the matter among the boys in certain public schools of Paris, and found that of those addicted to tobacco three fourths showed the palpable ill-effects in their pale faces, disordered circulation, weak muscles, and imperfect recitations; and the French Emperor was so impressed by the results of the inquiry that he at once issued an order totally prohibiting the use of tobacco by the students.

The devotees of tobacco are liable to suffer in many ways. The constant contact of the pipe or cigar with the lips and tongue sometimes produces the worst forms of cancer. Several cases of blindness, originating in the paralysis of the optic nerve, have been traced directly to the habit. Numberless cases of dyspepsia, or other derangement of the digestive organs, are traceable to the same source. Physicians report cases of genuine delirium tremens caused by excessive indulgence in tobacco. I have personally known one young man, a theological student, who was so far gone in that direction that he began to see little black objects wriggling about his pen when he attempted to write. Experienced medical men avow their conviction that the increased prevalence of paralysis and sudden death of late is, in a great degree, due to the increased use of intoxicating substances, including tobacco. In fatal cases of poisoning by tobacco death comes in the form of paralysis of the heart, the direct effect of the drug. Thus the enemy attacks the brain, the nerves, the digestive organs, the heart, and makes its deadly power felt in the very centers of life.

6. Tobacco sometimes prepares the way for alcohol, and the worst forms of intoxication.

This result does not follow, as it was once argued, because the mouth becomes dry by the use of the cigar, and thus a morbid thirst is created. The cause lies deeper. The system may be habituated to the mild intoxication and enslaved by it, and, in accordance with a fixed physical law, demands a constant increase of the daily portion in order to keep up the charm. And, to some at least, there comes a time when tobacco seems slow to do its work; the aid of a swifter, more powerful agent is invoked, and the victim drifts helplessly in the direction of still more dangerous narcotic indulgences.

7. Tobacco habits are expensive.

A gentleman of much experience in the business, proprietor of one of the largest manufactories of tobacco in the country, and well acquainted with the subject in all its parts, estimates the annual consumption in the United States at one hundred and twenty millions of pounds, costing those who consume it eighty-six millions of dollars. How can there be so large an aggregate expenditure without taking from many a laboring man a very perceptible portion of his earnings, and leaving him and his family the poorer in food, clothing, and daily comfort? Even among those who claim that they can spare what they thus spend, to what purpose is the waste? If a man limits himself to the small number of two ten-cent cigars a day, he needs to have just one thousand dollars, invested in seven-thirty bonds, to pay for them; and ten cigars a day require five thousand dollars in bonds. If he has no money to invest, then his habits have mortgaged him, soul and body, in that amount, and he pays the interest in daily installments. Could not the money be laid out to better advantage?

8. Tobacco habits tend to become fixed and tyrannical.

The victims all admit the danger of excess, but claim that they are "moderate" in the use, and mean always to be moderate. But here questions occur. What is moderation? Is it easy to maintain the limit which we set?

By confirmed, long-continued habit, tobacco becomes a necessity to the one addicted to it. His brain, his nerves, his whole system have become subjugated and enslaved, and without the powerful drug they are not in working order. Withhold the regular periodic indulgence, and there ensues first uneasiness and then distress. Every fiber in his body clamors for tobacco. In extreme cases the sufferer can neither eat, nor work, nor sleep, and his mental agony and confusion amount to incipient insanity. If an attempt at reform has created the trouble, the conflict is fearful. And in most cases the uneasiness, the tobacco hunger, the agony accumulates, like water in a mill-pond, till the dam breaks, the power of resistance fails, and every good resolution is swept away by the rushing flood. Men of intelligence and high moral character have told me, with tears, that they have tried to reform, and failed so many times that no heart or hope remains to try again. Is it wise carelessly to put on chains which in the end cut so deep?

If the reader has never acquired the habit of using tobacco, I would certainly advise him to stand fast in his present liberty. If he is somewhat addicted to the use, but thinks that he can stop at any time without an effort, I would suggest that now is the very time to do it. Should he continue to cultivate the habit, he may at some future hour make the humiliating discovery that if he would be free a fearful contest, a mighty agony, is before him. If he has already progressed so far that he feels he cannot escape without a fierce struggle with the appetite, I infer that the habit which so enslaves him is already doing him serious harm, and ought at once to be abandoned.

If any devotee of tobacco should object that this description of the difficulties of escape is overdrawn, my reply is, Try it. The dog tied to the axle of his master's wagon never finds out how strong the rope is till he begins to pull back.

Reform, however, is not impossible, and there are material aids which ought to be more widely known. Gentian root is not unworthy to be named here as a help in the good work. Possibly there are mysterious peculiarities of physical organization which prevent uniform results in all cases. One thing, however, is beyond dispute: inveterate chewers and smokers have been greatly aided by it in their battle for freedom. Carried in the pocket, and a small piece of it chewed from time to time when the old appetite is beginning to clamor for indulgence, it quiets the uneasiness, and in its general effect prevents that giving way of the whole nervous system, which is the chief difficulty in the way of an escape from the enemy.

CHAPTER VII.

THE HEMP INTOXICANT.

O that men should put an enemy into their mouths to steal away their brains! that we should with joy, revel, pleasure, and applause, transform ourselves into beasts.—SHAKSPEARE.

HEMP has long been known as a powerful intoxicant. Herodotus, twenty-three centuries ago, wrote that the ancient Scythians were addicted to the inhalation of the vapor of the burning plant. It seems from this that the practice of smoking the leaves is not a modern invention. Some writers conjecture that the *nepenthe* which Helen prepared for her guests was an infusion of this narcotic.

Hemp has been employed for centuries by the Turks as a luxury, and a procurer of abnormal mental states. It is said that during the Crusades the Saracens were accustomed to drug themselves to intoxication with it, and then with reckless fury make an attack upon the Christian army. The Turkish name of the preparation of hemp being *hasheesh,* and those addicted to the use of it being called *hashasheen,* it is supposed that the English word *assassin* originated in the time of these wars, and in the murderous deeds which the baleful drug instigated.

In some parts of South America, and also in Africa, as well as Asia, hemp is used in various forms and in large quantities. The plant possesses in all climates more or less of the narcotic property; but when grown under the burning sun of India it becomes peculiarly powerful. When the plant is in full growth a gum, charged with the poison, exudes from the tender stems and half-grown leaves. Sometimes the leaves and newly formed shoots are cut off and dried for use. Another mode is to boil the entire plant in alcohol, and thus extract its juices. The drug comes to market in various forms—a greenish paste, a dry powder, or simply as dried leaves. The leaves and flowers, smoked like tobacco, are highly intoxicating. Dr. Livingstone, the missionary traveler in Africa, thus describes the custom and its effects:

"The Batoka of these parts are very degraded in their appearance, and are not likely to improve, either physically or mentally, while so much addicted to smoking the *mutokwane*. This pernicious weed is extensively used in all the tribes of the interior. It causes a species of frenzy; and Sebituane's soldiers, on coming in sight of their enemies, sat down and smoked it, in order that they might make an effective onslaught. I was unable to prevail on the young Makololo to forego its use, although they cannot point to an old man in the tribe who has been addicted to this indulgence. Never having tried it, I cannot describe the pleasurable effects it is said to produce. Some view every thing as if looking through the wide end of a telescope; and others, in passing over a straw, lift up their feet as if about to cross the trunk of a tree. The Portuguese in Angola have such a belief in its deleterious effects that the use of it by a slave is considered a crime."

The Malays make a highly intoxicating drink by infusing the leaves, as do also the Hindoos. Like other intoxicants, it is joy, bliss, at the beginning, but ends in enslavement and ruin. The effects of a dose of the poison are very peculiar. Dr. O'Shaughnessey, a physician in the employ of the British Government in India, tried some experiments with it. For instance, he gave a rheumatic patient a grain of the resin at two o'clock in the afternoon. At four o'clock he was exhilarated in the highest degree. He talked incessantly, sang, and declared himself perfectly cured. At six o'clock he was asleep. At eight o'clock he was insensible, with the whole nervous and muscular system in such a state that, when the attendant lifted his arms and placed them in any given position they remained in the same posture, apparently without effort or weariness on the part of the patient. Brutes dosed with it are affected in the same singular way.

We are not confined, however, to the observations of mere spectators. Several travelers have tried the drug in their own persons, and have recorded their varied experiences. M. de Saulcy, while in Palestine, was curious enough to take a dose of what he afterward termed "the abominable poison which the dregs of the population alone drink and smoke in the East," and thus describes the result:

"We fancied that we were going to have an evening of enjoyment, but we nearly died through our imprudence. As I had taken a larger dose of this pernicious drug than my companions, I remained almost insensible for more than twenty-four hours; after which I found myself completely broken down with nervous spasms and incoherent dreams, which seemed to have endured a hundred years at least!"

Another physician, M. Moreau, tried the experiment with a different result, finding great enjoyment therein :

"It is really *happiness* which is produced by the hasheesh ; and by this I mean an enjoyment entirely *morale,* and by no means sensual, as might be supposed. The hasheesh eater is happy like him who hears tidings which fill him with joy ; or like the miser counting his treasures, the gambler who is successful at play, or the ambitious man who is intoxicated with success."

It must be remembered that the French word *morale* has no connection with what we term morals. The author just quoted is to be understood as saying that the enjoyment derived from a dose of hemp *seems* to be mental, and not physical. I call attention to the declaration, because in this feature of the effect hemp is but a type of the whole list of intoxicants. The cause is purely physical, and yet the impression, so far as it reveals itself to the victim, is wholly mental.

Another curious effect of the hemp poison is worthy of note. At a certain stage of the inebriation every thing toward which the eyes are directed seems to be enlarged to colossal dimensions. To the intoxicated negro, a twig looked like the trunk of a tree. Others tell us that the floor of an ordinary room appeared to spread out into a broad plain, so vast that it would require hours of travel to reach the other side. Duration also seemed to be extended in the same way, so that seconds appeared like hours, and hours became ages.

An American traveler, Bayard Taylor, when in Damascus, must needs be "silly enough," as De Saulcy expresses it, to experiment with hemp. He thus narrates the result. Through misinformation he took twice the usual dose, and yet for a time felt nothing, and began to conclude that the quantity taken was too small. But suddenly a strange thrill shot through him, and then another and another in quick succession. Then he seemed suddenly to grow to gigantic size. His whole being was filled with unutterable rapture; a bliss so deep, full, exquisite, that the very possibility of such happiness was a wondrous revelation. Visions rose before him. Now he was climbing the great Pyramid of Cheops. Now he sailed, in boat of pearl, over a desert whose sands were grains of shining gold, while the sky was filled with rainbows innumerable, the air was thick with delicious perfumes, and music, soft and entrancing, floated around him.

Suddenly the vision changed, and he fancied that he was a mass of transparent jelly, which the confectioner was trying to pour into a twisted mold. At this ludicrous idea he laughed till the tears ran down his cheeks; and lo, each tear became a loaf of bread rolling down upon the floor.

Then came a sudden change of the sensations. He felt as if on fire with fierce internal heat. His mouth seemed as hard and dry as brass, and his tongue felt like a bar of rusty iron. He seized a pitcher and drank long and deep, but was not able to taste the water nor feel its coolness. His sufferings grew more and more intense. In agony indescribable he stood in the middle of the room, brandishing his arms convulsively, heaving sighs that seemed to "shatter his whole being," and crying loudly for help.

Then he fancied that his throat was filling up with blood, which rose till crimson streams poured from his ears. Maddened by his agonies, he rushed out upon the roof of the house, and, as he did so, raised his hand to his head, and imagined that all the flesh had dropped off and left nothing but a hideous grinning skull. Turning back to the room, he sank down in measureless distress and despair. Reaction had come.

In all this Mr. Taylor dimly remembered who he was, and what he had been doing. But now a new horror was added. The fear came upon him that the poison had made him permanently insane, and that from the torments into which he had plunged there was no escape. At last he fell into a stupor in which he remained thirty hours; and when he began to awake it was with a system utterly prostrate and unstrung, his brain still clouded with visions, and all around him dim and shadowy. And thus he remained for days, scarcely noticing things about him, scarcely able to distinguish the real from the imaginary. Thus ended an experiment which came near costing life. It illustrates in an exaggerated form the whole process of inebriation, the dreamy, senseless pleasures of the first effect, and the horror, the wretchedness, which so soon buries in darkness and woe the memory of the previous fleeting enjoyment.

A few years ago a student of Union College, New York, became addicted to the poison, and, after his escape from the enemy, recorded his experience in a volume entitled "The Hasheesh Eater." He corroborates all that has been quoted from Mr. Taylor and Dr. Livingstone. The hemp intoxicant is a hateful poison. He who trifles with it sports on the brink of a gulf tossing with lurid fires and haunted with all shapes of evil.

Yet even the hemp intoxicant has apologists and defenders. Its victims indulge in it for a time with apparent impunity. They claim that it does them good, and that no evil follows, except in cases of excess. If rebuked for their degrading habit they offer specious arguments, like the victims of alcohol, and, in fact, make about as good a show of reason.

I will here add that the manufacturers of patent medicines here at home are using this abominable intoxicant in the preparation of their wares. This is no random assertion. Let the reader govern himself accordingly.

CHAPTER VIII.

THE OPIUM HABIT.

Now the serpent was more subtile than any beast of the field which the Lord God had made. And he said unto the woman, Yea, hath God said, Ye shall not eat of every tree of the garden?—GENESIS.

THIS most seductive and dangerous drug is prepared from the juice of the white poppy. India is the great producer of opium, the poppy being there cultivated in extensive plantations, and the drug exported thence to all parts of the world. The yield per acre is from twenty-five to forty pounds, worth there five dollars a pound. The annual trade of the East India Company amounts to ten or eleven million pounds of the drug, of which China is the leading consumer. The whole world uses opium as a medicine; and there is reason to fear that as an intoxicant its consumption is increasing even in Christian countries. The nations among whom it is used for the purpose of intoxication number four hundred millions of people.

This narcotic is used in three different modes. The liquid preparation, laudanum, and the way of using it, are too well known to need description. Among the Turks and the Chinese the solidified gum is preferred, some smoking it in little silver pipes, others swallowing it in the form of pills. In whatever mode it is taken, however, the effect is the same. A moderate dose allays pain, dispels care, and, as a rule, produces an indefinable exhilaration which men soon learn to prize very highly, and in it find great enjoyment. As in the case of other intoxicants, all persons are not equally affected, nor in the same way. There is a peculiarity of constitution which no one can explain, but by virtue of which a man is very susceptible of the intoxicating influence, his brain and nerves responding promptly, and the pleasurable exhilaration mounting to a high degree. Others get little or no enjoyment from the use of the drug, and are even made sick by it, without any indication of being intoxicated. Those who find that they cannot ascend the heights to which it lifts others have no reason to complain.

To get an idea of the effects of the opium habit when its mastery is fully established, we need but to turn our eyes to communities where it is openly practiced. As the hour for his daily dose approaches, the Turkish opium eater drags his emaciated frame slowly to the shop where he buys the drug, and, turning his livid countenance toward the vender, demands his customary dose, which is small or large, according to the length of time during which he has yielded to its sway. Clutching it with eager hands, he devours it, and then reclines upon a couch to await in stillness and silence the coveted result.

Soon new life begins to thrill along every nerve. His face flushes, his dull eyes brighten, his white lips grow red. He lies passive and inert, yet new power seems to him to steal into every muscle of his languid body, and inspire every faculty of his mind. He feels strong as Hercules, as bold as the desert lion, as eloquent as all the bards of Araby the Blest. His wild eye gazes upon floating visions of beauty and scenes of triumph. Now the observers see him half rising from his couch, and, muttering unintelligibly for a moment, sink down again. He imagines himself exalted before an entranced audience, pouring forth a rushing flood of words which sweeps all before it. The listeners hear him utter a prolonged moan ; he fancies that he is chanting a sweeter song than was ever sung by *houris* in Paradise. They see him writhe uneasily, and for a moment wave his hand feebly in the air ; he fancies that he is brandishing the saber of a mighty conqueror, cutting his way through hostile hosts, and winning crowns and empires by his valor.

But the spell begins to lose its power. It requires a space of time varying from one hour to two to reach the highest point of exhilaration ;

the dreamy ecstasy lasts from two hours to four, and then the visions fade till all is gone. Then comes a sleep which is not repose, an uneasy moaning sleep, with sudden starts and labored breathing. In three or four hours the opium eater wakes, wretched, wretched, wretched! His brain seems on fire, and yet his limbs feel heavy as lead. Gathering by degrees a little strength, he rises, swallows mechanically a little food, looks at the shadows of the morning, and groans as he thinks of the time that intervenes between the present and the hour of indulgence. Incapable of all rational thought or useful employment, he sits in sullen silence, while the slow hours wear away. As the period approaches, his appetite for the drug becomes more and more clamorous. His desire is as raging as a famished tiger's thirst for blood. To obtain it he would trample upon the bones of the Prophet; he would plunge his naked hand into molten iron. Though torment and death come with it, he must have it. And thus he goes on, day after day, month after month, constantly adding to the dose in order to reach each time the desired degree of intoxication, till at last the abused enginery of life gives way, and, suddenly as an extinguished taper, he dies.

In regard to the nature of the opium habit, we have the testimony of men of rare intelligence who were for a time its victims. Thomas De Quincey, the author of the "Confessions of an English Opium Eater," was enslaved by the drug for years. Suffering from a painful disease, he at length resorted to laudanum to obtain rest. He thus describes the effect of his first experiment:

"But I took it, and in hour, O heavens! what a revulsion, what an upheaving from its lowest depths of the inner spirit; what an apocalypse of the world within me. That my pains had vanished was now a trifle in my eyes. This *negative* effect was swallowed up in the immensity of those positive effects which had opened before me—in the abyss of divine enjoyment thus suddenly revealed. Here was a panacea, a φαρμακον νήπενθες for all human woes. Here was the secret of happiness, about which philosophers had disputed so many ages, at once discovered. Happiness might now be bought for a penny, and carried in the waistcoat pocket; potable ecstasies might be had corked up in a pint bottle, and peace of mind could be sent down in gallons by the mail-coach."

This language is doubtless extravagant, and the description very highly colored. Still, we cannot doubt that in some cases, at least, there is a high degree of enjoyment in the first experiences of an opium drunkard. On one point, De Quincey's laudations of opium are clearly at variance with truth. He claims for it great superiority over vulgar intoxicants. Wine, he says, unsettles the judgment, destroys self-possession, and calls into supremacy the merely human, or even brutal part of our nature; but the opium eater "feels that the diviner part of his nature is paramount; that is, the moral affections are in a state of cloudless serenity, and over all is the great light of the majestic intellect."

All this is delusion, a striking instance of the power to deceive which gives to all intoxicants treacherous charms. Let a man resort to an intoxicant of any kind, and just so far as he is affected by it, the efficient action of every faculty of the mind is disturbed and impaired. No greater error can be committed than to mistake for genuine mental vigor the imaginary strength which the victim fancies he sees exhibited in the unnatural workings of his benumbed brain.

A complete refutation of De Quincey's absurd positions is found in his own writings. He knew the effects of the drug; he knew all the stages of the downward path, from the first timid step to the final plunge into the gulf of despair and ruin. From the initial dose of thirty or forty drops of laudanum, which he took to lessen pain, he advanced to a daily consumption of eight thousand drops. He would sit down at night with a book, and a decanter of the poison, and sometimes not stir from his chair till morning, contemplating in silence the fantastic, dreamy imagery which floated along before the mental eye. He describes some of his visions, and, of course, gives us the best of them, and describes them in his best style.

Often his thoughts were busy for hours with a sort of mental panorama of which he could not trace the origin nor discover the meaning. He used to see mountains, plains, rivers, seas, oceans before him; sometimes oceans paved with human faces, "imploring, wrathful, despairing, which surged upward by thousands, by myriads, by generations." Frequently his sensations and mental impressions were horrible, but still unmeaning and unnatural.

"I was," he continues, "stared at, hooted at, grinned at, chattered at by monkeys, by paroquets, by cockatoos. I ran into pagodas, and was fixed for centuries at the summit, or in secret rooms. I was the idol, I was the priest. I was worshiped, I was sacrificed. I was buried for a thousand years, in stone coffins, with mummies and sphinxes, in the heart of eternal pyramids. I was kissed with cancerous kisses by crocodiles, and laid, confounded with all unutterable slimy things, among reeds and Nilotic mud."

One of the better sort of his reveries he describes at considerable length in language which is beautiful and eloquent, but indefinite, a true specimen of the cloudy sublime:

"It commenced with a music which I now often heard in dreams; a music which, like the Coronation Anthem, gave the feeling of a vast march, of infinite cavalcades filing off, and the tread of innumerable armies. The morning was come of a mighty day, a day of crisis and of final hope for human nature, then suffering some mysterious eclipse, and laboring in some dread extremity. Somewhere, I knew not where; somehow, I knew not how; by some beings I knew not whom, a battle, a strife, an agony was conducting—was evolving like a great drama or piece of music, with which my sympathy was the more insupportable from my confusion as to its place, its cause, its nature, and its possible issue. I had the power, and yet had not the power to decide it. I had the power, if I could raise myself, to will it; and yet again I had not the power, for the weight of twenty Atlantes was upon me, or the oppression of inexpiable guilt. Deeper down than ever plummet sounded I lay inactive.

"Then, like a chorus, the passion deepened. Some greater interest was at stake; some mightier cause than ever yet the sword had pleaded or trumpet had proclaimed. Then came sudden alarms, hurryings to and fro, trepidations of innumerable fugitives, I knew not whether from the good cause or the bad; darkness and lights, tempests and human faces; and at last, with the sense that all was lost, female forms, and clasped hands, and heart-breaking partings, and then everlasting farewells, and with a sigh the sound was reverberated, everlasting farewells; and again and yet again reverberated, everlasting farewells. And I awoke in struggles and cried aloud, 'I will sleep no more.'"

Where is "the light of the majestic intellect" in these crazy dreams? In all the revelations which De Quincey makes there is nothing "majestic," except the infinite assurance which seeks to palm off "great swelling words of vanity" as something highly intellectual.

The celebrated Samuel T. Coleridge is another example of the power to enslave which this dangerous drug wields over even the strongest intellects. He had been tortured for months with a swelling of the knees. Reading in a medical journal an account of a similar case which was cured by the use of laudanum, he tried it. At first it "acted like a charm," and for ten or twelve days he thought that his disease was gone. But it returned. Again laudanum was resorted to with success. But soon it was apparent, not merely that the drug must be continued to keep down the pain, but that to accomplish this result the dose must be increased from time to time. Thus, as he expresses it, he was "seduced into the accursed habit," and became an opium drunkard. One of the chief elements of peril in his case was the fact that an actual disease furnished an excuse with which to silence his own fears and throw him off his guard. While a new, artificial, but imperious appetite was growing, and he was fast sinking into a most degrading slavery, he thought that he was taking opium merely to lull his physical pain.

At last the fearful truth became apparent, first to others, and then to himself. His friends dealt faithfully with him, and with warnings and multiplied entreaties implored him to stop. He listened to all they said, confessed its truth, even with tears and groans, and kept on using opium. Yielding to their pleadings, he at last placed himself in the hands of a physician, and pretended to be gradually reducing his daily dose, while in fact he was secretly indulging in as large quantities as ever.

His friends, as the final resort, urged him to consent to be confined for a time in a private asylum for the insane. In reference to this project, imagine the shame and the anguish of a high-minded man who feels that he must in candor make this humiliating confession:

"There is no hope! O God, how willingly would I place myself under Dr. Fox in his establishment! for my case is a species of madness, only that it is a derangement, an utter *impotence of the volition* and not of the intellectual faculties. You bid me rouse myself. Go bid a man paralytic in both arms to rub them briskly together, and that will cure him. 'Alas!' he would reply, 'that I cannot move my arms is my complaint and my misery.'"

Coleridge did reform, however, though it cost him intense suffering. De Quincey also reformed after years of indulgence, but he escaped by no quick or easy process. Writing of the day when he felt that he could omit the dose and yet live, he says:

"I triumphed, but think not, reader, that therefore my sufferings were ended. Think of me as one, even when four months had passed, still agitated, writhing, throbbing, palpitating, and much in the condition of him who has been racked by the Inquisition."

The cases of these two eminent sufferers are given thus at some length, because they not only show the fearful power of the opium habit, the insidious way in which it approaches the victim, and the remorseless hold which it fastens upon him, but they illustrate the action of the whole list of intoxicants. How smiling the beginning, how silent and stealthy the growth; how heavy the chains become, and how they burn into the very flesh; how fearful the agonies of him who seeks to escape; how relentlessly the destroyer drags the prey down to his doom. While the effects of the various drugs used to produce intoxication are in some respects different, the general result is the same. The effects of the first indulgence upon a system ordinarily susceptible of the influence are agreeable, sometimes full of a new and exquisite enjoyment. By repeated doses, however, either the system adjusts itself in a degree to the drug, or else the brain and nerves become benumbed, and the dose which was amply sufficient at first fails to produce the dreamy joys which are the real object of desire. Therefore the quantity must be increased from time to time, and of this increase there is no end. The fifty drops of laudanum which spread rosy visions before the novice soon become a hundred; and the hundred, in time, become a thousand.

The slave of the habit sinks into a mental and physical wreck.

An intelligent traveler in Asia thus describes what he saw:

"A total attenuation of body, a withered, yellow countenance, a lame gait, a bending of the spine, frequently to such a degree as to assume a circular form, and glassy, deep-sunken eyes, betray the opium eater at the first glance. The digestive organs are in the highest degree disturbed, the sufferer eats scarcely any thing, and his mental and bodily powers are destroyed."

The Rev. S. L. Baldwin, who has been for ten years a resident of Foochow, describes opium smoking in China as a fearful and destructive vice. He estimates the smokers at four tenths of the adult male population, one third of the smokers being already enslaved and ruined, and the others gradually sinking into the same abyss. Intelligent natives regard the opium habit as the national vice, the great public enemy. The missionaries of all the Churches condemn the use of opium as a sin, and require total abstinence from it in converts. Reform is attended with good results of all kinds.

A native writer thus describes the effects of the habit:

"From the robust who smoke the flesh is

gradually consumed and worn away, and the skin hangs like a bag. Their faces become cadaverous and black, mucus flows from their nostrils, and tears from their eyes; their very bodies are rotten and putrid. It exhausts the animal spirits, wastes the flesh and blood, dissipates every kind of property, renders the person ill-favored, promotes obscenity, violates the laws, attacks the vitals, and destroys life."—*Chinese Recorder*, Sept. 1868.

Thus alcohol is the curse of one part of the race, and opium of another. A loud warning is needed even here in America, in regard to this pernicious drug. There is reason to believe that the use of opium as an intoxicant is increasing among us. There is ground for the suspicion that it enters largely into the composition of more than one of the patent medicines of the day. Even in cases of genuine disease, opium is too treacherous a thing to be used without the greatest caution. The use cannot be long continued without peril of fatal enslavement. For a little while the drug does no apparent damage and creates no alarm. On the contrary, the pleasurable sensations which it excites and which, in all their stages, are simply intoxication, may be mistaken for real increase of strength ; and the deluded invalid flatters himself that he is regaining his health, when the truth is he is adding a new disease to his original maladies, and his last state is worse than the first.

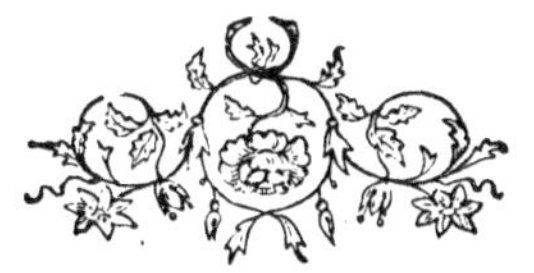

CHAPTER IX.

ALCOHOL: ITS PRODUCTION.

And the serpent said unto the woman, Ye shall not surely die: for God doth know that in the day ye eat thereof, then your eyes shall be opened; and ye shall be as gods, knowing good from evil.—GENESIS.

THIS powerful drug, in its various uses and abuses, has become the bane of the nations, both civilized and savage. Yet as the Turk who is given to opium defends his guilty pleasures, and calls the poison that ruins him "the gift of God," so in nations which boast of the greatest advancement alcohol has borne the name of the "water of life," while learning, eloquence, and poetry have taxed their resources to show that man's worst enemy, insidious, murderous, and relentless, is his best friend. In all ages, indeed, there have been wise men who saw the fearful evils which indulgence produces, and kept aloof from the destroyer; yet the race, as such, seems to have learned little from the woes through which it has passed, and cared little for the multiplied warnings given.

There have also been local triumphs of truth which cheer us with the hope of universal victory. Probably there does not exist among civilized men a population more free from the use of intoxicants than are the various bodies which constitute the evangelical Christian Church of the United States. But even here how slow has been the process of reform! how hard the contest which won the victory! There are multitudes yet living who remember when it was universally believed that alcoholic beverages were not only an innocent luxury, but a valuable aid in labors of every kind. The minister of the Gospel about to deliver his holy message, the lawyer about to make his final speech in an important case, thought that a few ounces of alcohol thrown into their veins would lend force to the brain, and give power and unction to the delivery. Firemen, with heroic energy and courage battling the flames hour after hour, did not doubt that alcohol gave them increased vigor and endurance. The farmer, going to his toil in the hot harvest field or the icy forest, imagined that with its help he could bear better both heat and cold. The physician, feeling the pulse of his patient, shook his grave head, and prescribed alcohol as a tonic to reinforce the feeble constitution; and in every family the prudent housewife kept a bottle of it among her collections of catnip and boneset and administered it, nothing doubting. It was regarded as a panacea, a grand remedy for all the ills to which flesh is heir, good for the young and the old, the rich and the poor, the strong and the weak, beneficial at all times and safe in all cases. Even now many imagine that alcohol has power to impart at least temporary strength to the body and vigor to the mind, and that it may, therefore, be resorted to with advantage to enable them to complete some weary task, or bear some sudden strain.

What, then, is alcohol, and what are its powers, its effects?

Alcohol is the product of a certain natural process called vinous fermentation. There are some facts, by no means new, which need to be repeated until they are universally known and felt.

So long as grain products or grapes and apples remain in a good state of preservation there is no intoxicating principle in them.

No art of the chemist can extract one ounce of alcohol from a thousand bushels of sound barley, or a thousand clusters of grapes, until the vital principle is killed and decay has begun. Nature has her methods of preservation, and when her apparatus is destroyed her golden treasures perish. Take, for instance, an apple as it ripens upon the tree. Its juices are so packed in minute air-tight cells as to be for a time secure from decay. Our mode of canning fruit is but an imitation. Every housekeeper knows that when the seal has been broken and the contents of the jar exposed to the air they must be used without delay or they will be spoiled. Crush an apple, and its myriads of cells are ruptured and its juices begin at once to decompose. The cider-mill does this work of destruction on a large scale, and the process of decay proceeds with equal pace.

The press is used to separate the juice from the more solid parts, or pomace; but I do not see how this separation either hastens or hinders the result. The process of decay goes on, the pomace rotting in one place and the juice in another. Nature is prodigal in her works, but economical in the use of her materials. When any organic body has lost its vital principle she proceeds at once to take it to pieces, that every atom which enters into its composition may be used in making something else.

In the apple as it hung upon the tree there was a saccharine element; and when the proccess of decay began, the atoms which composed the sugar entered into a new combination and formed alcohol. No vegetable substance will yield alcohol unless it has in it the saccharine element. The amount of alcohol depends on the amount of this element, a pound of sugar representing about half its weight in alcohol. Thus bland and pleasant food, touched by the fatal hand of decay, becomes a weapon of death.

The same thing is illustrated in the manufacture of an intoxicating liquid from barley. In its natural state, the living principle untouched, there is not a drop of alcohol in the whole harvest. But moisten the barley, and keep it at the right temperature, and in a little time the kernels swell and the germs start. The grain begins to grow, much as if it had been sown in the field. Just at this stage the grain is placed in the kiln, and its vitality is destroyed. It is now dead barley. Then it is placed in vessels and water is added, the mass being kept warm until the saccharine matter is dissolved. The liquor is next boiled, to complete the solution of the grain, and then is drawn off in vessels to ferment, and the result is the generation of alcohol. Thus, in the first case, alcohol is the essence of dead apples ; in the second, the essence of dead barley.

These two cases illustrate the methods by which alcohol is obtained from substances very diverse one from another. Wine is made from grapes and perry from pears, much in the same way in which cider is manufactured from apples. Treated after the fashion of barley, an intoxicating liquor can be made from Indian corn, wheat, rye, or even potatoes. Mead, or metheglin, which was long the favorite intoxicant of northern Europe, is made of honey, three times its bulk of boiling water and a little yeast being added, and the mixture allowed to ferment. In their representations of their heathen heaven the warrior is described as reclining at his ease, drinking mead from the skulls of his enemies. Not many years ago its manufacture was not unknown in some parts of our own country. It is said that a person drinking a certain quantity of this honey beer is able distinctly to hear swarms of bees buzzing in his head.

The Tartars make an intoxicating beverage from milk, the sugar of which is changed to alcohol by fermentation. West India rum is made of molasses, which is diluted with water and allowed to ferment. The negroes of Africa find the means of intoxication in the fermented juice of the palm-tree. They make an incision in the bark and collect the sap which flows from it, and which ferments and becomes alcoholic. The same custom obtains in India, in the South Sea Islands, and, in fact, wherever the palm-tree grows. In Mexico the natives make an intoxicating drink of the fermented juice of the century plant, or American aloe. A full-grown plant yields from one to two gallons of sap daily, and the flow continues two or three months. In twenty-four hours the *pulque* is ready for use. I do not doubt that the sap of the sugar maple, treated in the same way, will ferment and become alcoholic.

In all the beverages named, derived as they are from many various substances, the intoxicating principle is the same. In proportion to the amount of alcohol which it contains, each of them is intoxicating. Moreover, all these beverages owe their supposed value to alcohol alone, and without it could no more create the fictitious enjoyments which they impart, nor wield their strange power to deceive and destroy. Science utters this declaration in no uncertain way; and we place it among the facts which ignorance and presumption alone will assail, or pretend to doubt.

DISTILLATION.

The art of separating alcohol from the various compounds into which it enters seems to have been known among the Arabians some time before it made its way to the nations of western Europe, but where or by whom the process was invented cannot now be determined. The first distinct reference to it dates back to the thirteenth century, when we hear of it among the alchemists who were seeking the philosopher's stone.

Our business, however, is not to trace the superstitions and follies which clustered about it then, but to show its bearing upon the present times. There is still error in the popular idea. Alcohol is the product of fermentation, and of no other process. Distillation never created one drop of alcohol since the world began. Distillation merely sifts out the alcohol already present in the mixtures subjected to the process.

There is little mystery in the operation. For example, cider is about one tenth alcohol, the rest being water, clouded by certain solid matters, and having the peculiar taste which reveals its origin. Alcohol boils at 173 degrees of Fahrenheit's thermometer, while water requires a heat of 212 degrees. Consequently, if cider be subjected to heat the alcohol in it will boil first. This is the whole secret. The distiller boils cider in a closed vessel, from the top of which extends a long metallic pipe, which traverses a cistern of cold water. The trick consists in keeping up the fire just to that degree which will cause the alcohol to boil, but not the water. The alcohol passes in a state of vapor along the pipe, is condensed on its cool inner surface, and runs into a vessel prepared to receive it. When the alcohol has all passed over the watery residue is thrown away.

In this way alcohol can be separated from the various beverages of which it forms an element. Distill wine, cider, beer, ale, metheglin, the fermented sap of the sugar-cane, the palm-tree, or the agave, and the result is the same. And when the alcohol is gone, the most ardent devotee of the original drink turns with disgust from the flat and powerless residue. Take the alcohol from ale, and there remains only a poor, weak vegetable soup. Take it from lager-beer, and the residue is only a very thin gruel. Take it from any of the various beverages of which it forms a part, and not only is the power of mischief at once gone, but the charm, the exhilaration, the supposed virtue, is fled, and not a vestige remains of all the excellences which its admirers attribute to it.

Consequently, when men addict themselves to alcoholic beverages it does not make as much difference as some imagine to which they shall have recourse. If one man drinks brandy, the alcoholic strength of which is fifty per cent., and another prefers cider at ten per cent., and the latter consumes five gills where the other drinks one gill, the result, both in theory and practice, will be the same. If, in the process of cultivating the habit, the victim finds that he can attain the happiness he seeks only by means of the stronger intoxicants, it merely shows that his brain and nerves are so benumbed by the drug that his veins will not hold enough of the weaker sort to intoxicate him.

One word here in regard to our domestic wines, made, as the simple housewife says, of "nothing in the world but currants and a little sugar." The sugar is added to increase the quantity of alcohol. The necessity for the addition arises from the lack of saccharine matter in the pure juice of the currants. There is some, but not sufficient to generate alcohol enough to make the wine "keep." Currant wine is alcoholic, as well as others.

CHAPTER X.

ALCOHOL: ITS DELUSIONS.

We are nae fou'; we're no that fou',
  But just a drappie in our e'e;
The cock may craw, the day may daw,
  And aye we'll taste the barley bree.

BURNS.

THIS branch of our investigation is not easy to pursue. We want to know how a man feels with alcohol in his blood, and how shall we ascertain? We are indeed surrounded by a great cloud of witnesses who ought to be able to inform us; but, unfortunately for our inquiry, few of them have cared to watch closely the effect of their potations. Cool, accurate, thoughtful men are not apt to indulge in intoxicating drugs. It is hard to find a man who has not only had a thorough experience, but has retained his mental power and his habits of close observation, and is willing, for the benefit of others, to tell what he knows.

There is a story of an enthusiastic French physician who, when a fearful plague, a new and terrible disease which baffled the skill of the profession, was raging among the people, voluntarily exposed himself to the contagion, and then shut himself up to die alone, carefully noting every symptom of each stage of the malady till the pencil dropped from his hand. We need similar information in regard to alcoholic intoxication, but where shall we find it?

For what do men drink alcohol? When they invoke the powerful drug, what effect do they anticipate and desire? What is the effect upon the mind? What is the effect upon the bodily powers? The mere statement of a few of the points to be investigated reveals the difficulty of the task.

When a man is susceptible of the true narcotic influence the primary effects are marked and definite. In such cases alcohol creates an animal happiness which is more or less exalted according to the quantity of the drug employed, and the promptness and completeness with which the brain and nerves respond to its action. We are so constituted that it is not possible at all times to draw the line between mere physical sensations and the experiences which belong wholly to the mind. It is not improbable that there may be found among the victims of alcohol those whose sense of pleasure is greater in the incipient stages of intoxication than in any part of their sane life. The glowing descriptions given of the joys of opium and the hemp poison will doubtless apply, in a good degree, to those of alcohol. It will be remembered that M. Moreau describes the effect of hemp, not as a sensual pleasure, but *happiness*, a state in which the mind itself is filled with an exalted enjoyment akin to that experienced by the man who has just heard very good news, or achieved some great success.

Thus alcohol creates in the man himself an

impression that he is stronger, warmer, wiser, keener, and more witty than in ordinary times. If he is working at some weary task, whether of mental or physical labor, it seems for the moment to diminish the fatigue. If he is in pain, it relieves it. If he is in trouble, it lifts him out of its reach. If he is exposed, hour after hour, to the snow and fierce wintry winds, it seems to help him to endure the cold. If called to make a public address, it enables him to face the audience with less trepidation, and to deliver his sentiments, as he thinks, with more force and effect.

De Quincey affirms that his first experiment with opium revealed to him possibilities of enjoyment of which he did not know till then that he was capable. Taylor's trial of hemp produced in him the conviction that there exist in our being depths and heights which common life seldom reaches, perhaps never. A wise man will respect these mysteries of his own nature, and be in no haste to fathom them. He will quietly wait till the divine hand, either in this world or that which is to come, shall disclose the full capacity of the human instrument, and call forth its richest harmonies.

It is very possible that the vivid descriptions of De Quincey and Taylor are somewhat exaggerated. It is also certain that alcoholic intoxication is less intellectual, and of a lower, more animal type generally, than that of opium and hemp; still the effects are similar. Alcohol, as well as the drugs named, has power to intoxicate, to create a physical rapture, an indefinable happiness, which, for the time, sweeps the whole current of thought and emotion into new channels, and reigns supreme. All experience proves this, whether the evidence is sought among savages or sages, philosophers or poets. Dr. Edward Smith, of London, has published the results of certain experiments which he tried upon himself and his friends. He thus reports:

"Spirits made us very hilarious and talkative

in ten minutes, and during twenty to twenty-five, so much so that my friend was altogether a king. But as minutes flew away, so did our joyousness; little by little we lessened our garrulity and felt less happy, until at length, having gone down by degrees, we remained silent, almost morose, and extremely miserable."

A well-known literary celebrity, Charles Lamb, says in his Letters:

"My habits are changing from drunk to sober. Whether I shall be happier or no remains to be proved. I shall certainly be more happy in a morning; but whether I shall not sacrifice the fat, the marrow, and the kidneys, that is, the night, glorious, care-drowning night, that heals all wrongs, pours wine into our mortifications, and changes the scene from indifferent and flat to bright and brilliant, is a question."

Robert Burns, a very competent witness, thus paints the mental condition of his hero, Tam O'Shanter, as he sat with his comrades in the village ale-house, getting intoxicated:

"The night drave on wi' sangs and clatter,
And aye the ale was growing better.
The souter tauld his queerest stories,
The landlord's laugh was ready chorus.
The storm without might rair and rustle,
Tam didna mind the storm a whistle.
Care, mad to see a man sae happy,
E'en drowned himself amang the nappy.
As bees flee hame wi' lades o' treasure,
The minutes winged their way wi' pleasure;
Kings may be blest, but Tam was glorious;
O'er all the ills of life victorious."

This animal ecstasy may be so great as to overpower all reality, and compel the whole mental action in its own direction. As heavy winds blowing against the current of a broad river sometimes prevail over it for a brief space, and even drive the waters backward, so the wild joys which alcohol produces may be potent to overcome sorrow, anxiety, and disappointment, and give the soul an hour of rest from the burden.

Let our poet again testify:

" 'Twill make a man forget his woe;
'Twill heighten all his joy;
'Twill make the widow's heart to sing,
Though the tear were in her eye."

The relief is indeed but momentary. The realities of life remain unchanged. The woe of the man is no less ; the widow is a widow still ; and soon the spell will be dissolved, and the sorrow and the loneliness return. The waters which were stayed for a season flow again in accumulated volume. The floods lift up their voice, and out of the depths the sinking soul cries in deeper anguish. Nevertheless, when the victim is in a good degree susceptible of the true alcoholic influence, and is not too far gone in his career, the pleasure, I doubt not, is intense. The unthinking drink of a magic fountain before unknown, and the unhappy are cheated into temporary forgetfulness of their grief, and lifted into a delusive peace and happiness.

And herein lies the fatal power of the whole list of intoxicants. They are cheats, impostors, mockers. They exalt men to a state of high mental enjoyment which has no foundation in reason or reality. The miser, counting his piles of shining gold, is happy ; but the beggar with a gill of alcohol in his veins may be just as happy. The ambitious man, whose long cherished hopes and far-reaching plans are at last crowned with success, feels a thrill of pleasure as he contemplates the result of his efforts ; but his happiness may be poor compared with the dreamy raptures of the man whose whole life has been a failure, but whose brain is just now under the spell of a poisonous drug. Take the victim of misfortune, defeated, dispirited, his courage all gone, and lay the enchantment upon him, and, lo, he is transfigured. His bowed form becomes erect, his dull eyes brighten, his pale face flushes, his sadness gives place to smiles, and his moody silence to laughter and song. He ceases to feel weariness and pain ; he forgets his diffidence and caution ; he remembers poverty and grief no more. On his new-found wings he mounts above them all, and revels in the clouds. And, strangest of all, the man who seems to possess little intellect, little sensibility, small capacity for either joy or sorrow, sometimes appears to rise as high in this animal exhilaration, and be as happy, as those accredited with better gifts and greater powers of every kind.

With this forgetfulness of sorrow, this sensuous bliss produced by alcohol, another curious effect follows. The physical enjoyment blends with the mental action, and colors every view which a man takes of himself, his possessions, and his conduct. As in music, when we hear a beautiful or touching song fitly sung, we forget to draw the line between that part of the pleasure which comes from the sentiment, and that which comes from the mere sound, so he who is under the influence of alcohol often attributes to other sources the enjoyment which really springs from the intoxicant alone.

When a company of men are drinking together they tend, at least for a time, to be talkative and merry, and the feeblest attempt at a jest is greeted with unlimited laughter. There may be no affectation in their merriment. The joke really seems to them unspeakably comical; but they are not conscious that their appreciation of it is greatly intensified by the fact that, before it was uttered, they were feeling very funny indeed.

So if one of the company takes it into his bewildered head to try to reason about something, he is, in his own eyes, a veritable Solomon; and, if he is talking on their side of the question, his equally bewildered comrades marvel at his supernatural sagacity and eloquence. As one intoxicated with hemp sees a great tree in every twig which lies in his path, and distances of a few yards stretch into imaginary leagues, so to the man intoxicated with alcohol any poor pebble of forced wit is a sparkling gem, and every puddle of muddy discourse has ocean depths of wisdom in it.

Nor does the deception pertain only to the advanced stages of the process of inebriation. I am persuaded that from the beginning to the end the mental effect is in nature the same.

When the victim has become visibly intoxicated, and rendered himself the derision of the unfeeling, he openly betrays effects which closer observation would have detected at the beginning, long before his speech became indistinct or his gait unsteady.

After examining the subject with all the aid which I have been able to obtain from every quarter, I find myself driven to this conclusion, that alcohol cannot give to a well man even temporary vigor either of body or mind, and that the ideas prevalent on the subject are based on a wrong interpretation of facts. There is no borrowed physical strength or endurance. There is no borrowed mental brilliancy. There is, indeed, an animal joyousness which makes the man under the influence of the drug feel strong, and wise, and acute; but this proves nothing in favor of the intoxicant. It is notorious that this delusion is at its height when mind and body both are fast sinking into the imbecility of the last stage of intoxication.

Thus alcohol stands indicted as an impostor. He who is fully under its influence may be happy after a fashion, but his enjoyment is based upon a mockery. He feels like a giant, while he is really shorn of his natural force. He drivels the veriest nonsense, while he thinks he reasons better than Plato. His maudlin attempts at smartness are the feeblest and the flattest of human utterances; but they seem to him wit almost superhuman. When he is so far gone as to stammer in his speech and totter in his gait, and be helpless in mind and body, his sense of his wisdom, his strength, his greatness, and his goodness is at its highest point.

10

CHAPTER XI.

ALCOHOL: ITS REAL EFFECT.

Wine is a mocker, strong drink is raging: and whosoever is deceived thereby is not wise.—PROVERBS.

THE effect of alcohol upon the human organism has, within a few years, been examined with a scientific accuracy and thoroughness before unknown. The wonder is that physiologists have been so slow to recognize the importance of the subject, and devote to it the patient observation and careful research which the public welfare demands. It is a cause of rejoicing that attention has at last been called in this direction; and that, in both Europe and America, there is a manifest disposition to examine matters anew from the foundation.

We are especially indebted to MM. Lallemand and Perrin, of Paris; Doctors Anstie,

Chambers, Brinton, and Smith, of London; and Dr. N. S. Davis, of Chicago, who have devoted much time to the investigation, and have gathered facts from which a consistent theory may be constructed.

MM. Lallemand and Perrin, aided by the celebrated chemist Duroy, conducted a long series of careful experiments instituted to ascertain the effects of alcohol on the human organism. After pursuing the investigation for years, they sum up the result in seven formal statements:

1. Alcohol is not food.

2. Alcohol exerts a special influence over the nervous system, a small dose acting as an excitant, a larger one as a stupefiant.

3. Alcohol is neither changed nor destroyed in the human organism.

4. Alcohol accumulates by a sort of elective affinity in the brain and the liver.

5. Alcohol is eliminated from the human organism, unchanged in nature and undiminished

in quantity, the channels of escape being the lungs, the skin, and the kidneys.

6. Alcohol has a direct and serious tendency to produce disease by the development of functional disturbances and organic changes in the brain, the liver and the kidneys.

7. Spirituous liquors derive from alcohol their common properties and their special effect.—*Du Role de l'Alcohol,* page 233.

The latter part of the second item may need to be stated more accurately. The animal ecstasy and the dulling influence attend, in their degree, doses of every size; but in the case of small doses the exhilaration is the symptom which attracts most forcibly the attention of observers, while in the case of large doses both mind and body succumb so soon to the paralytic influence that the observer perhaps fails altogether to detect signs of the peculiar sensuous enjoyment which alcohol produces.

With the second item accurately stated, these conclusions are to be regarded as the latest verdicts of science. Here, then, we stand on the rock. Alcohol taken into the stomach is speedily absorbed and poured into the blood. Thus it makes its way to every part of the system, especially the brain, and every-where it is alcohol, unchanged and unchangeable. If we eat a piece of bread or beef, the finer particles are gathered up and poured into the blood, and carried to every part of the body as material for growth or for repair. The very atoms of which the food consisted are built into bone and muscle, brain, nerve, every organ and every tissue. But alcohol stays nowhere, because it is not building material. It is not digested nor decomposed. It departs in various ways, by the breath, by the perspiration, and otherwise, but it is still alcohol. The French experimenters killed dogs with heavy doses of the drug; and then, dissecting them and applying the appropriate tests, found that pure alcohol could be distilled from the blood, the brain, the flesh, and every part of the body. Repeating a part of their experiments on human subjects, they found the effects the same.

Dr. Christison, of Edinburgh, a very high authority in medical questions on both sides of the Atlantic, says of the peculiar effects of the drug: "The sedative action of alcohol on the brain constitutes it a powerful narcotic poison."

Dr. Anstie takes the ground that what we call intoxication is an incipient and temporary, but real, paralysis of the brain, and that ether, chloroform, alcohol, and certain other substances, have the peculiar property of producing this result. He denies that there is even temporary invigoration of body and mind, but affirms that every power is dulled from the first moment of the visible effect. In his investigations he reached "one distinct conclusion, the importance of which appears to be very great; namely, that, as in the case of chloroform and ether, the symptoms which are commonly described as an evidence of excitement, depending on the stimulation of the nervous system preliminary to the occurrence of narcosis, are in reality an essential part of the narcotic, that is, the paralytic influence."—*Stimulants and Narcotics*, page 415.

"This palsy of the brain is responsible for all the so-called 'mental excitement.'"—Page 408.

Dr. Davis says: "Numerous chemical analyses of the blood and different tissues, made by different experimenters, show that when alcoholic drinks are taken the alcohol enters the blood, and permeates with it every part of the body. While in the blood, and circulating through the system, alcohol diminishes the sensibility of the brain and nervous system in the same manner as other anæsthetics."—*Nature of Inebriation*, page 3.

But this conclusion ought not to rest, nor does it rest, upon the bare assertion of men, however eminent in their profession. It rests upon facts. And perhaps I ought to say, in justice to my position, that it was taken, and the proofs of its correctness were set in order, before I saw Dr. Anstie's elaborate work, or knew of Dr. Davis's investigations. The ascertained and acknowledged facts in regard to the action of alcohol compelled me to the conclusion that it is not a stimulant as popularly accounted; that a well man cannot borrow from it for one hour either augmented bodily strength or mental force and brilliancy; and that we have mistaken for these effects an animal happiness, a sensuous rapture, which is wholly consistent with the dulling of every sense and the decline of every mental and every physical power. What, then, besides the animal rapture and its accompanying delusions, are the effects of alcohol upon men in good health?

1. The Animal Heat declines.

For a time, the doctrine prevailed that alcohol undergoes in the lungs some change whereby heat is generated. More thorough investigation, however, proves this an error. Experiments made by Dr. Davis in 1850, and repeated in 1867, fully establish the fact that heat declines. The following report of one experiment will illustrate. Three doses of the drug, one gill each, were administered to a well man at intervals of thirty minutes, the temperature of the blood and the rate of circulation being carefully noted:

Time.	Temperature.	Pulse.
10 30 P. M.	98¼	83
11 "	97¾	85
11 30 "	97½	89
12 30 "	97½	85

The pulse, indeed, increased in frequency, as the figures show, but the force declined. And, as Dr. Anstie remarks, "Increase of frequency always implies debility when coupled with diminution of force."

Professor Bing, of the University of Bonn, in Prussia, has recently investigated this question, and published, among other conclusions, that "The heat of the body is always lowered by alcohol; and alcohol preserves life in febrile affections, where the temperature rises very high, by its cooling properties."

The fact stated by Professor Bing is not to be

doubted. His inference is not so clear. May not the cooling influence of alcohol in cases of fever be but one element of a more general effect? So little is really known on the subject that I feel at liberty to suggest that in such cases the good effect of alcohol may arise from its sedative action on the whole system, whereby the morbid irritation is allayed and a period of comparative repose is secured, during which the vital forces rally, somewhat as they do during healthy sleep.

With the pulse falling off in force, and the animal heat decreasing, how can alcohol, as some fancy, aid men in enduring extreme cold? Experience, as well as theory, denies this. Arctic navigators affirm that in cases of exposure alcohol increases the danger. An eminent northern explorer, Sir J. Richardson, says, "I am quite satisfied that spirituous liquors diminish the power of resisting cold." It is said that in the Russian army, when a long march is made in very cold weather, the soldiers are forbidden to drink alcohol, because it would render them more liable to be frozen.

Nor must we rush to the opposite conclusion, that alcohol, exerting a cooling influence, must therefore be good in hot climates. That which tends to diminish the normal action of vital forces is bad every-where. Sir Charles Napier, in May, 1849, addressing his English regiment at Calcutta, said, with soldierly emphasis, "Let me tell you that you are come to a country where if you drink you are dead men." The gallant Havelock, too, who gained an immortal name during the rebellion in India, declared that "water drinking is the best regimen for a soldier." The experience of the crews of American vessels making voyages to tropical ports, the experience of European laborers sent to build railways in the West Indies, is to the same effect.

2. Alcohol lessens Physical Strength.

The fact already shown renders inevitable the decline of bodily force. While the blood is cooled below the normal point, the strength must of necessity be lessened. This is proved, not by mere inference, but by the accurate observations of scientific men.

Dr. Chambers, one of the most eminent men of his profession in England, alluding to the supposed power of the poison to impart at least temporary strength, says:

"It seems very doubtful if, on the healthy nervous system, this is ever the effect of alcohol, even in the most moderate doses, and for the shortest periods of time."

Dr. Brinton, of London, declares that "Careful observation leaves little doubt that a moderate dose of beer or wine will in most cases diminish the maximum weight which a person can lift." The conclusion of MM. Lallemand and Perrin is that "muscular power is weakened" by alcohol.

But if the drug is not only unable to lend men temporary vigor, but actually lessens it, much less can it impart permanent strength. This is the verdict of the ages. Two thousand years ago the Greek athletes who were training for the various contests at the Olympic games rigidly abstained from wine. The prize-fighters of our own day follow the same rule, abstaining not only from alcohol, but even from tobacco. On no other terms can the highest physical condition be secured.

The Oriental traveler, Mr. Buckingham, says "that the finest race of men he saw in India were a tribe living among the Himalaya Mountains. They had never tasted alcohol in their lives; yet in feats of strength the best men, among the British soldiers and sailors at Calcutta, were no match for them."

E. P. Weston, who has taxed human strength and endurance to the utmost in his long journeys on foot, declares, that in attempting feats of this nature "the use of intoxicating liquors is not only unnecessary, but wholly injurious."

There is a reason for all this. Alcohol is not food. All action involves a waste of the tissues. There can be no real permanent addition to physical strength where there is no physical renewal. Alcohol in the human system enters into no new combination of any kind. It is recognized as an intruder and an enemy, and is cast out of the body as speedily as possible by every available channel.

3. Alcohol disturbs the Action of the Senses.

The sight, the hearing, the sense of touch are less acute, less accurate and reliable, from the moment the intoxicant begins to operate.

The evidence of our invaluable witness, the poet Burns, is not to be despised because it assumes a humorous form.

> "The village ale had made me canty;
> I was na fou', but just had plenty;
> The rising moon began to glower,
> The distant Cumnock hills out-owre;
> To count her horns wi' all my power
> I set mysel;
> But whether she had three or four
> I couldna tell."

Not only do the joints in the floor, and the straight edges of the stones in the pavement, seem to writhe like serpents before the eyes of the inebriated man, but the vision, the hearing, the touch, are affected long before there is any visible inebriation. A gentleman of intelligence, who had in his early life some little experience on these points, informs me that he often noticed when he drank a glass of brandy that, almost instantly, the senses were impaired, so that if he laid his hand upon any object he did not feel it quite as distinctly as before, and that sight and hearing were perceptibly hindered, although in a way very difficult to describe.

A physician of more than ordinary skill related to me an experience which occurred to him some years ago. On his way to visit a patient whose disease was not yet determined, and whose case he desired to examine with all possible care, he was seized with sudden illness. Although in principle and practice an abstainer, he was induced to stop at a hotel and procure a small quantity of brandy. It did not produce the slightest outward indication of inebriety;

vet, when he reached the bed-side of his patient and tried to proceed with his diagnosis, he was surprised to find his senses so dulled by the dose as to unfit him for the nice observation requisite for the occasion. What he experienced in that particular case Dr. Brinton, in his work on Dietetics, asserts as a rule:

"Mental acuteness, accuracy of perception, and delicacy of the senses are all so far opposed by alcohol as that the maximum efforts of each are incompatible with the ingestion of any moderate quantity of fermented liquid. A single glass will often suffice to take the edge off both mind and body, and to reduce their capacity to something below their perfection of work."

For twenty years Professor Davis, in his lectures at the Medical College of Chicago, has taught the doctrine that "alcohol is simply an anæsthetic, a sedative to nervous sensibility, and debilitating to all the physical functions." As such, it differs from ether and chloroform, in that the effect lasts through a longer period. It is sometimes used as an anæsthetic by practical men. I am well acquainted with an experienced and skillful dentist who, in tedious, painful operations, sometimes employs alcohol in preference to ether or chloroform. A gill of whisky dulls mind and body, lessening both the nervous apprehension and the actual pain. Another practical illustration may be given. A gentleman who now abhors his former errors told me that one day, while wild with drink, he dashed his fist through a window, cutting himself fearfully, yet he felt no pain whatever.

It may be added that rope-dancers, and others who perform feats of the nicest skill, in which the slightest tremor of the nerves, the momentary failure of the hand, the eye, the judgment, would not only mar the performance, but imperil life, dare not drink a single glass of any intoxicating beverage when about to commence their exhibitions. Again, not the theories of the mere scientific inquirer, but the stern experience of practical life, teaches us a lesson.

This benumbing of the organs of sense, occurring as it does under circumstances which show that the effect is not local but general, reaching outward from the nervous centers, is of itself evidence that the brain also is benumbed and in a state of incipient paralysis.

4. Alcohol disturbs the Mental Action.

On this point Dr. Anstie makes the following observation :

"The early phenomena of alcoholic intoxication usually wear an appearance at first sight much resembling excitement. But on analyzing the symptoms, we are at no loss to perceive that it is the emotional and appetitive part of the mind which is in action, while the intellect, on the contrary, is directly enfeebled."—*Stimulants and Narcotics*, p. 78.

All the facts show that under the influence of alcohol the entire nervous system is dulled, partially paralyzed. How, then, can the intellect fail to be affected ? That it is greatly enfeebled during the advanced stages of the process of intoxication all admit; and the facts, correctly interpreted, show that the enfeebling effects may be detected at the very beginning of inebriation, while, as yet, exhilaration is the chief symptom manifested. Dr. Anstie himself tried a small dose of alcohol, and in a very few minutes found his pulse beating more rapidly, felt a degree of numbness in his lips, and was conscious of a confusion of thought.

The inebriating process cannot go far before the mental effects become evident. Just in the degree to which the exhilaration mounts, cool judgment and rational self-control are lost, caution is lulled to sleep, the dread of pain and the sense of danger are forgotten, and the mind is filled with a false consciousness of strength, wisdom, and courage. We again avail ourselves of the evidence of the Scotch poet:

> Inspiring, bold John Barleycorn!
> What dangers thou canst make us scorn!
> Wi' tippenny we fear nae evil;
> Wi' usquabae we'll face the Devil!

5. Alcohol wars with Moral Self-control.

This result is inevitable, from the effects already shown. While the mind is dulled, and caution lost, and the dread of evil destroyed, a man cannot be expected to conduct himself wisely and well. The theory once was that an intoxicated man is apt to rush into folly and crime, because the intoxicant inflames his lower passions and makes them ungovernable. This may or may not be the case. There is something decidedly animal in the alcoholic exhilaration; but the controlling power being for the time disabled by the drug, the brutish part of human nature would assert itself more strongly even if not specially influenced. The beasts of the menagerie may be no fiercer than before, but they rage more violently and are more dangerous because the cages are open and the keepers are gone.

The lower passions being thus left without a master, the tendency to evil of every sort is greatly augmented. Any spark of temptation is liable to start a conflagration. Anger, malice, revenge, every destructive passion rages, because the palsied mind feels only the evil impulse, and cares nothing for consequences. The daily records of every criminal court, every page of the daily journals, illustrate this statement. Under the bewildering power of this baneful drug the bad become worse, the cruel more cruel, the sensual grow brutish, and those who might otherwise maintain their integrity fall an easy prey to the tempter.

But it may be said that certain facts militate against the theory advanced. Men who use alcohol declare that it does aid them—that it does lend them temporary vigor, both mental and physical. They drink, and feel wiser, better, braver, stronger, more eloquent than before. Byron and Burns are said to have written some of their wittiest productions under alcoholic inspiration; and famous names of later times and nearer home could be cited to show that eloquent oratory may owe something to the same agency. Talfourd, the biographer of Charles Lamb, referring to the habits into which his friend had unfortunately fallen, says, "Drinking, with him, was not a sensual, but an intellectual pleasure. It lighted up his fading fancy, enriched his humor, and impelled the struggling thought or beautiful image into day."

The traveler facing the cold north wind, the laborer toiling on in some emergency twice the allotted hours of hard work, are as confident as men can be that alcohol helps them, at least for the time. How shall we reconcile with the experiences of actual life the facts which science and observation have demonstrated?

The reconciliation is not difficult, because there is no real conflict. When a man has long been addicted to indulgence in alcohol his general condition is disordered, diseased, so that when he is deprived of his daily allowance his nerves are unstrung and the whole man is in distress, and in this condition he can do nothing well. In such a case it is not to be denied that the drug which is ruining him, and for which every fiber of his body is clamoring, has power to quiet for the time the physical distress and the mental agitation, and enable him to do what in his morbid condition he otherwise could not do.

The inveterate drinker of alcohol seems to borrow intellectual brilliancy and force from his cups; but it is only because his whole system is enslaved and diseased, so that, without the aid of his treacherous ally, he is totally unnerved and powerless. What he would have been if he had never fallen into bondage is another question. It is safe to say that mind is always obscured by alcohol, and that those who seem to derive most temporary aid from it would, if free from their enemy, be capable of far better things than the best productions of these hours of delusive vigor.

Alcohol may also lend apparent mental brilliancy to men who ordinarily tend to be silent in the company of others. It lulls caution, it overcomes diffidence, it unfits the mind to weigh surrounding circumstances or to criticize closely its own productions ; the feeling of exhilaration hurries the timid man into speech, and he seems to borrow from the narcotic both fertility of thought and ease of expression.

Nevertheless, the mocking beverage has really created nothing. While it has loosed his tongue, it has added no mental force, no mental treasure. The very utmost that the drug can do is to utter the magic *sesame* which bids the rocky doors of the cave open and reveal something of the wealth already gathered there.

It may be added here that we unconsciously tend to overestimate the wit or the wisdom of a man who is under the influence of alcohol. We do not expect him to be either witty or wise, and therefore we wonder at it the more. We listen in something of the frame of mind with which we witness the performances of the Learned Pig, or the feats of the Educated Mules.

Moreover, if the mental force be really augmented, even for the hour, what becomes of the prevalent idea that men drink to drown care and trouble? If there be true stimulation, then the mind would be roused to a more intense activity, the sensibilities would be more acute, and every care and trouble be apprehended still more clearly, and felt still more intensely.

In regard to the apparent augmentation of physical strength and endurance, the explanation is equally easy. When the laborer is worn out with toil, every muscle protests against abuse. The sense of weariness gives warning. There are two ways of silencing this voice: one is to cease work and let the weary rest; the other is to pour into the veins a drug which deadens the nerves and thus quiets the uneasiness, and at the same time fills the mind with a dreamy sense of happiness which buries all unpleasant sensations as he continues his toil. Still, no strength has been secured. The overtasked muscles are no better prepared than before for continued exertion. When the drug ceases to operate he will feel as completely worn out as he would have felt if he had worked the whole time without the alcohol. The whole gain in the case, by the use of the drug, arises simply from the deadening of the nerves, so that, for the time, they utter no complaint against abuse. He borrows from the intoxicant not temporary force, but temporary insensibility.

So in the case of the traveler exposed to extreme cold. His hands, his feet, begin to ache, and the wintry winds seem to search his very bones. He pulls out his flask, drinks, and declares that he feels warmer. But what is the reality? The animal heat declines under the influence of the intoxicant, and he is in greater danger than ever. But alcohol has partially paralyzed his whole system, his deadened nerves give no warning, and the man in his delusion concludes that the danger is gone because the pain has ceased. It is the old story of the ostrich, which, when pursued by the hunter and just on the point of being taken, buries its foolish head in the sand, and thinks that it has escaped from the enemy.

In fact, while the devotees of alcohol have been laughed at for ages because they resort to it for help under the most diverse and contradictory circumstances — when they are cold and when they are hot; when they are wet and when they are dry; when they are working hard and when they are weary of doing nothing —they have acted in a much more philosophic way than they have had credit for, seeing that alcohol deadens the senses and the sensibilities, and tends to bury unpleasant impressions of every description.

Thus Alcohol, with his treacherous face hidden under a smiling mask of friendship, marches at the head of his murderous band. All crime, all shame, all shapes of horror and despair, disease and death, follow in his train; while Humanity, Patriotism, and Religion weep as they contemplate his triumphant career.

CHAPTER XII.

ALCOHOL: THE HEREDITARY EFFECT.

Visiting the iniquities of the fathers upon the children unto the third and fourth generation.—Exodus.

THERE is in the minds of observant, thoughtful men a suspicion, and more than a suspicion, that the evil consequences of an abuse of intoxicants do not always end with the original offenders. I do not now refer to the want, the neglect, the brutality, which are often sources of cruel suffering to those whose sad heritage it is to be the children of inebriates. These things lie upon the surface, and thrust themselves before our eyes at all times.

But there are woes infinitely worse than these. There is reason to believe that the child sometimes inherits from drunken parents constitutional effects and tendencies which darken life from the beginning and fill it with fearful dangers. In a Report upon Idiocy made to the Legislature of Massachusetts by Dr. Howe, an eminent physician who has made this and kindred topics his study for years, we have this remarkable statement: "The habits of the parents of three hundred of the idiots were learned, and one hundred and forty-five, or nearly one half, are reported as known to be habitual drunkards." One case is cited in the report, where, both parents being inebriates, seven idiot children were born in one family. The reputation of Dr. Howe is a sufficient voucher for the accuracy of the facts and figures given. Nearly one half of these poor imbeciles, then, are the offspring of intemperate fathers and mothers.

But no State in the Union has a nobler or more powerful army of the friends of reform. Nowhere has the cause of temperance achieved nobler triumphs. The intemperate adults of Massachusetts form but a small part of the whole number. The State contains about six hundred thousand adults. Even if we assume that twenty thousand of these are inebriates, they constitute but one in thirty of the whole number. But Dr. Howe's figures show that this small minority of the population have nearly as many idiots born to them as have the majority. Taking, therefore, equal numbers of temperate and intemperate parents, the intemperate have nearly twenty-nine times as many idiots among their children as do temperate parents. We cannot question the statements of the report. We cannot deny the truth of the inference.

Statistics gathered in other lands point to the same conclusion. In Norway, in the early part of the present century, the production of ardent spirits was restricted by severe laws. In 1825 the restriction was removed, and in a very few years the number of the insane was twice as great as before in proportion to the whole population, while the number of idiotic children born had increased in a still greater ratio.

But great evils may be inherited where there is no apparent lack of intellect. If inebriety in the parent can be visited upon the child to the almost total loss of mental power, we can readily believe that it may operate to the depravation of the body, and the production of mental peculiarities and evil tendencies. On this point Dr. Joseph Parrish of Pennsylvania, who has for many years studied with great care the subject of intemperance and its effects, thus remarks of a certain class of patients:

"They may possess intellectual or moral obliquities, or be deranged by positive disease, or by physical organizations for which they are not wholly responsible, and which a wiser philosophy than now obtains will some day trace to their pre-natal history."

Dr. A. N. Dougherty of New Jersey, in an address which he delivered, and which was afterward published under his own supervision, thus puts on record his deliberate judgment in the case:

"There are, unhappily, many, very many persons born with a proclivity, a natural aptitude, to indulge in intoxicating liquors, which only needs favoring circumstances to be developed into fatal activity. Their parents have transmitted to them this among other constitutional tendencies. As scrofula, as pulmonary consumption, as gout, as insanity comes by inheritance, so does this."

Dr. Carpenter of London, a physician of the highest authority in England, quotes with approval the remark of Dr. Hutcheson, of the Glasgow Lunatic Asylum, in regard to the periodic form of intemperance: "It is frequently hereditary, being derived from a parent predisposed to insanity, or addicted to intemperance."

Quotations to the same effect could be multiplied indefinitely. These, however, will suffice to show the convictions of men who are not only eminent authority in their profession, but have given special attention to this very subject. They do not, indeed, assert that the child in all cases inherits from the intemperate father an uncontrollable proclivity for intoxicants. Such an assertion would not be true to the history of families. Young men whose parents are gross offenders against the laws of sobriety may grow up free from the vice. This is especially apt to be the case where there is a mother of intelligence and high moral character to wield a saving influence over her children, and also endow them with her own better nature. Nevertheless, this does not invalidate the principle. The fact cannot be disputed. Where one parent is an inebriate, the child is, in a certain degree, liable to inherit constitutional peculiarities which increase the danger of his becoming a prey to the same remorseless destroyer. Where both parents are intemperate, the danger is still greater.

Example doubtless aids in the work of death. The son sees the father drink. The means of indulgence are constantly at hand. He hears none of the warnings which fall upon the ears of others. The natural curiosity which makes children eager to taste of what they see others eating or drinking prompts him to watch for chances to get at the object of desire, and the first trial may impart so much pleasure that he is more eager for it than ever. Thus by degrees a decided taste is acquired, and the foundations of an evil habit are laid.

But, as we have seen, there is more than the force of example and opportunity to surround with peril the unhappy children of the inebriate. They are apt to inherit, not only a feeble constitution, exposed to the inroads of disease, but also peculiarities and tendencies of such a nature that the love of an intoxicant easily fastens upon them. It may be difficult to explain the precise character of these peculiarities. As in natural science there are ultimate atoms which can neither be dissolved nor divided by force, so in reasoning we find ultimate truths which we recognize as such, and all attempts at explanation are useless. Why calomel should affect the liver and not the wrist is not clear Why lead poisons should affect the wrist and not the liver no mortal can show. Why there should be here and there a patient upon whom opium or quinine will not act in the usual way no physician can tell.

And as no human science can tell why the general effects of alcohol are what we find them to be, so no man can explain its diversities of action in individual cases. I am persuaded that there is an inexplicable peculiarity of organization, by virtue of which the possessor is unusually susceptible of the true alcoholic exhilaration. His brain and nerves respond freely to the narcotic, and he mounts into a state of high sensuous enjoyment. He soars, he exults, he triumphs! His whole being is whelmed in rushing floods of pleasure, which bury care, pain, and sorrow in their depths. Another may drink an equal amount of the same intoxicant and find no enchantment in it. We cannot tell the reason. Men in their folly see marks of greatness each in his own peculiarity, the one class claiming a finer organization, and complacently construing their susceptibility as proof of genius; the other with equal complacency interpreting their slowness to respond as evidence of mental strength and manly vigor, saying to those who wisely decline to imitate their Bacchanalian excesses:

> "Thy bane is in thy shallow skull,
> Not in my silver bowl."

All this is weak and pretentious vanity. Neither those who get the highest inspiration from alcohol, nor those who fail to be even exhilarated by it, have any occasion to plume themselves on their superiority. That a man is inebriated by half the amount of alcohol usually necessary for the purpose is no better evidence of an organization favorable to the display of talent than is the fact that he may require only half the usual quantity of calomel when in need of that medicine. That another man should require twice the usual quantity of alcohol to intoxicate him is no better proof of mental strength than would be his needing twice as much of the calomel.

From all the information which I have been able to gather on this point, I infer that men of equal mental and physical stamina may be unequally susceptible of alcoholic exhilaration. Consequently some are in greater danger than others where the perils from without are the same. Two young men may take their first glass together, and the one be wrought up to a wild ecstasy, while the other gets no sensuous enjoyment, and wonders at his comrade. It is easy to see which of them will be tempted to repeat the experiment. Give the two a daily dose for a month, and it is easy to conjecture upon which of them the habit will fasten with firmer hold. Those who are in a high degree susceptible of narcotic exhilaration are as tinder, where alcohol is fire. The first taste sometimes applies the spark and lights an unquenchable flame. That children should inherit from their parents this constitutional susceptibility seems as natural as that they should resemble them in the color of their eyes.

I am persuaded, also, that the man who is constitutionally the slowest to respond to alcoholic influence may, by long continued use, be so enslaved by the intoxicant as to be uneasy, or even in extreme suffering, without it. His habits have wrought a physical change in him. They have created a morbid condition of the nervous system, so that it seems to him impossible to live without the aid of the poison. A few hours' abstinence suffices to fill him with an agony of desire which often sweeps him along in defiance of his clearest convictions, and in violation of his most solemn vows.

Nor is this morbid condition of the system a mere transitory thing. It may last for years after the use of the intoxicant has been totally abandoned. Many a victim has reformed, and maintained his integrity for so long a period that he began to fancy that he was as safe as if he had never fallen. Trusting in the completeness of his recovery he has ventured to drink a single glass of wine, and the first taste has roused the insane appetite in all its old fury, and the good work of years has been undone in a moment. And among the reformed there are wise men who are aware of all this, and dare not taste alcohol even as a medicine, knowing well that even to look at it and inhale the odor would be in the highest degree unsafe. If, therefore, so deep and permanent is the work wrought in the human constitution by the continued use of the intoxicant, what hope is there that the evil will not tend to be hereditary?

And facts are not wanting to show that parental transgression may entail upon the child a peculiar and most fearful peril. When a man has long indulged the evil appetite, and then reformed, he may be troubled years afterward by the recurrence of burning desire. There are times when he is restless, uneasy, and no healthful food nor ordinary drink will satisfy his wants. He knows well whence his restlessness originates, and, if wise in the wisdom of this world, he avoids with anxious care every thing that would fan the kindling fires; if wise in the wisdom of the other also, he looks to the Strong for strength. What creates his trouble and renews the old battle for life? Is it because he has not yet forgotten the joys of indulgence? The cause lies deeper. The conflict is thus renewed from time to time, because his system has never yet really recovered its normal condition.

Dr. Livingstone, the missionary explorer, tells us that the Africans believe that a man bitten by a lion never fully recovers, but to the day of his death is subject to periodical rending pain in the wounded place, as if the fangs of the monster were again fastened in his flesh. It seems to be so with the man who has been wounded by alcohol. And the saddest fact of all is that his innocent children may inherit his scars, and feel the sharp teeth of the devourer.

They may be born not only with the dangerous susceptibility of alcoholic influence, but with organizations perverted and depraved by the vice of the parent, so that they too have their paroxysms of morbid restlessness and undefinable longing, when no employment contents them, no pleasures already known to them attract, no healthful food or drink satisfies, but when the first casual taste of the intoxicant thrills them with insane rapture, and marks them for a mad career and a doom from which all human tenderness and pity toil in vain to save them.

CHAPTER XIII.

ALCOHOL: THE WRONG OF INDULGENCE.

Drunk, and speak parrot and squabble? Swagger, swear, and discourse fustian with one's own shadow? . . . To be now a sensible man, by and by a fool, and presently a beast. O strange!—SHAKSPEARE.

IF no damage remained after the pleasure is gone, the use of an intoxicant for the sake of enjoyment would still be essentially degrading. What is a man seeking when he flies to the fountains of intoxication? If he could be candid with himself, he would see that the effect at which he aims is really a mental effect; that he seeks to disturb the regular action of reason, memory and conscience; to immerse his whole being in fictitious happiness; to withdraw the soul for a time from contact with the rough realities of life, and give it, while the spell lasts, an insensibility to evil, and a delusive pleasure which belong not to it in its natural, rational state.

And how does he propose to do this? He accomplishes it by turning traitor to his own nobler nature, by taking advantage of the union of the mortal with the immortal to wrest the soul away from true activities, and wrap it in an unreal enjoyment which has no connection with the aim or the successes of his life, his hopes or his fears, but comes from the action of a poisonous drug. He seizes upon the body, and by its abuse fills the mind with dreams and surrounds it with false lights and shadows, giving it a visionary life from which it must soon awake to find itself without courage or strength, and to which it will be tempted with fearful power to return, that it may escape the sense of shame and the goadings of remorse. Can we imagine a habit more unnatural, more degrading, more ruinous, more unworthy of the life which we ought to live, and the destiny which we every moment approach? If, therefore, the effects of the intoxicating cup could be confined entirely to the moments in which it wraps the soul in pleasant delirium, it would still be a degrading source of enjoyment.

But the effects are not confined to the hours of delirious pleasure. They darken all the hours that follow. Opium, hemp, alcohol are essentially poisonous, nor can they be indulged in habitually without injury. Just so far as the habit has become strong and the demand for the intoxicant imperious the system is diseased. A brain and nerves in a healthy natural condition do not clamor for alcohol, opium, or tobacco.

The damage begins as soon as the foundations of the habit are laid. For a time, possibly for a considerable time where the habit forms slowly, the injury may not be so revealed as to compel the victim to confess it. Health is subject to a thousand attacks, great and small, few of which we are able to trace directly to an open enemy, and nature's first warnings of the growing evil are lost in the general confusion.

But sooner or later wronged nature utters a cry which cannot be misinterpreted. In the victim of coca, the sallow skin, hollow eyes, and idiotic expression of the face are merely outward tokens of a general decay. The Turkish opium eater, the Chinese opium smoker, who totters feebly along with bent form, making wild gestures and muttering insane things as he goes, is only reaping where his own hand sowed. And the unhappy inebriate of our own kindred, with his bleared and watery eyes, his foul breath, diseased body, and clouded intellect, a poor human wreck, broken down in mind and soul, in happiness, reputation, and estate, in the things of this life and that which is to come, has merely reached the point toward which he has been traveling with steady step from the hour of his first indulgence.

When the ship is wrecked the cargo is never safe. When sin ruins the body the immortal mind cannot escape. The reason becomes weak and unreliable, the memory fails, the will loses its force, and every power of the intellect is impaired. The injury begins with the formation of the evil habit, and progresses as the habit grows. No man who seeks exhilaration in the use of a drug, however little of the intoxicant it takes to secure it, can possess while under its influence the same cool reliable judgment which he would have if he were free from his enemy.

The moral nature also suffers. There is a principle involved here which deserves more than the brief allusion which we are able to give it. The Creator has adjusted our mental and emotional nature to our circumstances and our needs. It is in accordance with the divine purpose that when we succeed in a worthy undertaking we shall feel elated ; when we fail, depressed. It is by design that when we do wrong we experience shame, fear, and remorse, and when bereavements come we sorrow. Thus our impulses and emotions correspond to the facts of our life, and are meant to rouse to present duty, cultivate in us some valuable element of character, or foreshadow the eternal future with its awards.

But by means of intoxicating drugs all this may be changed, so that the heart swells with delusive joy when no worthy deed has been done; and no shame or remorse is felt however shameful and wrong the conduct, no sorrow experienced however great the bereavement. Opium or alcohol has power, at least for a time, to take away the pain, the sorrow, the mental suffering which the Creator intended to follow certain actions or accompany certain events, and in the place thereof fill the soul with a wild, unreal, irrational happiness.

Consequently, by means of intoxicants the adjustments of the moral world are deranged, put out of joint. A man with alcohol in his veins is not the man that God made. He has not the sense that God gave him, nor the conscience that God planted in him, nor the tender affections and sensibilities which God bestowed upon him. He has reconstructed himself after another model, which, so far as it differs from the original, is marred, perverted, distorted—not what Divine Wisdom intended or what man's true interests demand.

Under the influence of the drug, a man not naturally worse than others can do unworthy deeds, and feel no warning pang of self-condemnation; he can do a cruel, brutish act, and feel no pity for the one who suffers. He can stain his hands with blood and rush into foulest crime without one thought of human justice or divine retribution, the penalties of sin in this life or the life to come. It is, therefore, an enormous sin against God, against himself and his fellow-men, which a man commits when he yields to be enslaved by an intoxicating poison. The habit unmans the victim, lessens every moral and rational safeguard, and increases every dangerous tendency in his nature. When the intellect is clouded, the sensibilities dulled, the moral nature paralyzed, and the animal passions no more under the control of reason and conscience, the conduct cannot fail to be foolish, brutish, or devilish, or all three by turns. All observation shows that just so far as men fall under the tyranny of an intoxicant they are unfitted for the responsibilities of life, and become dangerous to themselves and to each other.

Nor is the reign of evil limited to the brief periods during which the tides of insane rapture bear upward. The system becomes in time so perverted by the habit, that, if the narcotic is withheld, the nerves are unstrung, and the whole body craves the drug with a burning agony of desire which makes men reckless, desperate, mad. Then there is a new and powerful plea for indulgence. The unhappy one rushes on to excess, not to secure pleasure, but to escape suffering; not to scale the flowery heights which once rose before him, but to avoid plunging into a black abyss which he knows is opening just behind him. Charles Lamb, in a confession written "with tears trickling down his cheeks," thus describes this condition:

"I have known one in that state, when he has tried to abstain but for one evening, though the poisonous potion had long ceased to bring back its first enchantments, though he was sure it would deepen his gloom rather than brighten it—in the violence of the struggle, and the necessity he has felt of getting rid of the present sensation at any rate—I have known him to scream out, to cry aloud, for the anguish and the pain of the strife within him. Why should I hesitate to declare that the man of whom I speak is myself?"

Thus the process goes on, in every depth a lower deep. The brain and nerves become so diseased that the constant use of the intoxicant is a necessity. The absence of the narcotic effect results in untold wretchedness. We read with profoundest pity the stories of shipwreck and starvation; and when we find the famished survivors ready to sustain a miserable existence by feeding upon the bodies of the dead, we accept the horrid deed, not as evidence of the deeper depravity of the wretched men who do it, but as the measure of their indescribable sufferings. A little of the same charity is not wholly out of place in interpreting the mad career of the slaves of narcotic indulgence.

We have seen how desperately Coleridge struggled for his life against the tyranny of opium. His powerful intellect weighed well the motives to reform, and saw clearly the dark gulf into which he was plunging. Hosts of friends gathered about him to strengthen his faltering determination, and aid him with words of cheer; yet he was ready to cry out, "There is no hope," and give up the contest. But when was a sadder experience ever told than that which is contained in these touching words of Lamb:

"The waters have gone over me. But out of the black depths, could I be heard, I would cry out to all those who have but set a foot in the perilous flood. Could the youth to whom the flavor of his first wine is delicious as the opening scenes of life, or the entering upon some newly discovered Paradise, look into my desolation, and be made to understand what a dreary thing it is when a man shall feel himself going down a precipice with open eyes and a passive will—to see his destruction and have no power to stop it, and yet to feel it all the way emanating from himself; to perceive all goodness emptied out of him, and yet not be able to forget a time when it was otherwise; to bear about the piteous spectacle of his own self-ruin; could he see my fevered eye, feverish with last night's drinking, and feverishly looking for this night's repetition of the folly; could he feel the body of the death out of which I cry hourly with feebler and feebler outcry to be delivered—it were enough to make him dash the sparkling beverage to the earth in all the pride of its mantling temptation."

We wrong the fallen one when we denounce his apparent lack of honor, and every noble attribute, and refuse to recognize the strength of the chains which bind him, the weight of the iron hand which drags him to his doom. The sailor, starving on his poor raft, knows what a horrid deed he is doing when he mutilates the body of his dead comrade and devours the flesh; but he is mad with hunger. The inebriate too knows well what he is doing, but he is maddened by an appetite as fierce and relentless as that of the perishing victim of famine. He sees deep sadness settle like evening shadows upon the faces which he loves. He knows that as he falls fond hearts are breaking. He weeps, and prays, and resolves, and struggles with his foe in mighty agony. But a grip of steel is upon him, and a power which he cannot resist hurries him onward. The resolutions of one hour are scattered as chaff the next, and on he goes through dishonor, and sorrow, and wrong over the ruins of character, happiness, and hope, over the bleeding forms of innocence and love, trampling upon human compassion and God's law, and the divine mercy, and heaven's offered peace, till the grave swallows up his ruined body, and darkness unfathomable and eternal engulfs his ruined soul. And cruelest, foulest wrong of all, the evil which he does may live long after he is gone, repeating itself in his children, born with the shadow of death upon them.

And what is there to offset this appalling catalogue of evil? What pearl of great price is bought at this infinite cost? Absolutely all that is gained by the beginner is an occasional hour of delusive, sensuous pleasure which ends in gloom and pain. All that the veteran finds is a brief period of rest from a gnawing appetite which takes a new lease of life from each indulgence, lays hold of its victim with a tighter grasp, and bites with a sharper tooth. Is it wise to pay so much for so little?

CHAPTER XIV.

ALCOHOL: THE FOLLY OF BEGINNING.

Then the devil taketh him up into the holy city, and setteth him on a pinnacle of the temple, and saith unto him, If thou be the Son of God, cast thyself down: for it is written, He shall give his angels charge concerning thee,—MATTHEW.

WHAT alcohol, in the hands of a competent and conscientious physician, may accomplish I will not undertake to determine. The doctors disagree among themselves, one party holding the opinion that it is a valuable aid in certain cases, and indispensable in general practice; the other affirming that occasions seldom occur where it can be used to advantage, and that even then its place can be supplied by other means without detriment to the patient. It is safe to say that the field in which alcohol is thought to be of service is much smaller to-day than it was fifty years ago, and little is risked in the prediction that it will be prescribed by the safest and best practitioners of medicine with still more caution in the years to come. It does not concern the friends of reform to deny its place in the *materia medica.* In fact, the more clearly it is proved to have a place there, the more evident it becomes that it does not belong among safe and useful articles of daily consumption in time of health. All medicine is detrimental to us when we are well. The course of treatment which makes the sick man well would make a well man sick. The same dose which wakes action in some torpid organ would hurry the healthy one into morbid activity. The same drug, by means of which the patient gains an hour's respite from pain, would sink the man free from suffering into a lethargic sleep from which he would wake in pain, and with his system all in disorder. Prove, then, that alcohol is a medicine, and the same reasoning proves it detrimental to men in health.

And this is the unanimous verdict of those who have given the question a thorough examination, and spoken their honest convictions. To persons in the enjoyment of good health, the use of intoxicating beverages is not only useless, but detrimental and dangerous. If those who are addicted to the intoxicant in any of its diversified forms are disposed to doubt, let them open a regular book-account with their habit. Let them set down to the credit of alcohol all the good it really does them, estimated on the most liberal scale which truth will allow. Let them set down on the other side the cost and the loss of every kind, not forgetting to examine the value of the vast interests involved. Let them add to this a valuation of the peril incurred, not measured by their estimate of their own wisdom and power of self-control, but by the general average of evil done in the community by these same habits. Can any man be so blind as not to see how the account stands?

Alcohol benumbs the brain, dulls the senses,

lessens the physical force, darkens the intellect, diminishes the power of conscience and the capacity for self-control, impairs every element of true efficiency, multiplies dangers on every side, and attacks our interests in every direction. A man in a state of gross intoxication feels as strong as Hercules, and "wiser than seven men that can render a reason;" and every simpleton who happens to see the sight makes himself merry over the folly of the inebriate. But while the man who has only an ounce of the intoxicant in his veins, and who experiences only a slight measure of consequent exhilaration, is laughing or sneering at another who reels and drivels under the influence of four ounces, is he aware that in his degree he too is cheated, and that the augmented mental and physical vigor which he thinks that he feels is in his case, as well as the other, an utter delusion?

It is certain that in every stage of the process of inebriation the whole action, mental, moral, and physical, is disturbed, so that the intellect is less sure, the sensibilities less tender, the lower passions less subject to control; and the man is more liable to commit errors of speech and of conduct and to fall before temptation, less able to encounter disease or the extremes of heat and cold, less capable of anything which requires quickness of intellect, calm judgment, nice manual dexterity, or great endurance.

Nor can any man indulge in the habitual use of an intoxicant without danger. Not only is excess ruinous, but what men in their folly term moderation is unwise and wrong. What is there to prevent "the moderate use" from being "moderately" injurious?

Again, moderation, so called, is not a level rock upon which the feet may be firmly planted, but a declivity, steep and slippery, at whose base lie dead men's bones. By a law as fixed as that which holds the planets in their orbits, it is impossible to adhere to a certain definite allowance of the intoxicant, and at the same time continue to gain the object for which the drug is used. The man addicted to opium or alcohol aims to secure by its help a degree of exhilaration, a sensuous happiness, which will render him oblivious of the ills of life, and lift him out of the shadows into the sunshine. But the fifty drops of laudanum, or the ounce of alcohol, which answered the purpose at the beginning, soon fail to exalt to the required height. The nervous system either adjusts itself in a degree to the power of the drug, or loses its sensibility, and requires more to affect it. Hence there is a constant demand for an increased quantity, a steady pressure urging the victim to cross the line which he has drawn. If he resists and maintains the limit, the daily portion ceases to exhilarate in the way and to the extent which he desires, and the habit asserts its power chiefly in the unrest, or the sharp suffering, which the omission of the daily allowance creates. The allowance then must be increased from time to time, or the enjoyment will lessen and finally cease. The votary of forbidden pleasures can no more reverse this law, or escape its operation, than he can escape from the law of gravitation.

The chances are all on the side of increase. By continued indulgence the unnatural appetite daily grows stronger and more imperious. This morbid craving is not satisfied till the due degree of exhilaration is reached. To stop short of it is only pain, disappointment, aggravation. But while the forces which impel onward have been growing stronger, the power of resistance has been declining. What men call the moderate use of alcohol dulls the mind, deadens the sensibilities, lessens the controlling power of the conscience and the will, and renders the whole condition weak and insecure. What probability is there that the man who has been so unwise, so careless of his own welfare, as to fall into the habit of daily taking a poisonous drug to secure a delirium of sensual pleasure, will be able to resist successfully when an increase of the quantity is demanded? To cling to the original amount, and on each occasion to halt at the edge of the coveted enjoyment, the very borders of the Land of Promise; to do this steadily and persistently day after day is infinitely more difficult than entire reform, involves a greater degree of self-denial, and requires a greater force of resolution.

Some, indeed, maintain themselves in this trying position for a time. Some do it for long periods when circumstances are favorable. But let the horizon grow dark with disappointment and disaster; let loss and care and sorrow come, and then the rule which was to stand forever is apt to be forgotten, the line is passed, and a new and worse stage of the dangerous journey is reached. Thus the habit silently, secretly, day after day, contends for the mastery, missing no chance to conquer by a sudden blow, crushing out every hope, and riveting fetters which cannot be broken. Coleridge, the slave of opium, and Lamb, the slave of alcohol, confess the humiliating, appalling fact that the power of self-control declines at every step in the downward road, and at length seems totally destroyed.

He, then, who deliberately decides to attempt a "moderate use" of intoxicating beverages deliberately resolves to run all these risks. In one of the fables of old Æsop the lion reproaches the fox for not coming to see him when he was sick; and the cunning animal replies that he did come as far as the mouth of the den, but, happening to cast his eyes upon the ground, he observed that the sand was full of tracks, all of which pointed inward, and he concluded to go no farther.

The lair where the alcoholic monster waits for his prey is not destitute of foot-prints which point outward, but many of these show the unequal impressions made by the wounded; many are stained with blood. And great hosts, uncounted myriads, have never returned. Not only have the gay, the young, and the heedless been lost in the dark den, but the wise, the strong, the great have fallen into "the ever grinding jaws!" Why name the fallen? They are found every-where. The farmer, the mechanic, the merchant, the physician, the lawyer, the statesman, and even the minister of the Divine Word, have felt the fatal fascination, and died "as the fool dieth."

Some of them doubtless possessed the dangerous susceptibility of alcoholic influence which made it almost certain ruin to attempt any use of the intoxicant. And some at first found little pleasure in the cup, but persevered until they established in themselves an artificial necessity for it. They all had doubtless their seasons of penitence and remorse, and their spasms of reform, but finally despaired, and yielded to their fate.

He who decides to attempt "moderation" determines to try to stand in a slippery path, where multitudes which no man can number have fallen. He resolves to abandon the safe and solid rock, and encounter the storms and whirlpools of a treacherous sea whose shores are strewn with wrecks.

And still other perils await him. Indulgence generally begins in social ways, and when a man realizes the danger and seeks to escape, powerful social influences array themselves against him. In the gay circles of fashionable life, to refuse to do as others are doing, is not only to confess personal danger, but to give offense, break the tacit compact, and chill the genial warmth of pleasant companionships. He must adhere to old customs, or look for new friends.

In the more common walks of life, strange as it may seem, the professed friends of the victim are generally the first and the most active in opposing his efforts to escape his doom. Conscience tells them that what he is doing, they too should do, and the warning is unwelcome. His determined course reproaches their irresolution. Every day he maintains his high resolve, convicts them of weakness, and fills them with shame. And so, watching, plotting, sneering, coaxing, using all manner of ingenious and cruel devices, they labor to draw him back to ruin.

And there is one who watches him with the keen eye of the vulture, and sees with deep dismay every true and lasting reform. I would not denounce any man unjustly; but every vender of intoxicants knows well what his success in business will cost the community. He grows rich by the poverty of others; he lives by their death. He must have customers. To win them, he smiles and flatters; provides games, newspapers, and perhaps music. To render his place the more attractive to the idle, he, in some cases, secretly pays some coarse and noisy humorist a salary to frequent his house, and play the decoy to lure the flock within his reach.

And when he has secured a crowd sufficient to support him in ease and indolence, how can he fail to be alarmed at any movement which threatens to scatter it? Thus he who would burst the chains of evil habit must expect his old associates to assail him on every side, de riding, reproaching, and soliciting by turns. He must expect to find the mercenary dealer in intoxicants plotting in cold blood to ruin him, and trying by all manner of mean and treacherous devices to accomplish it. And all the time this outward conflict is going on, the vicious appetite within, held down by main force, but not yet slain, is clamoring for indulgence like a famished lion roaring for his prey.

How can he maintain his resolution with all this flood of evil influences surging against him? Truly the wonder is, not that so few, but that so many succeed.

The Koran tells us that the bridge by which true believers pass from earth to Paradise is no wider than the edge of a sharp saber; and the path by which some try to cross the great gulf of alcoholic excess is quite as narrow. To sum up the whole matter, four facts are established:

1. To men in health the use of alcoholic beverages can do no good of any kind whatever.

2. Under the continued use of alcohol the

sensibility of the nervous system declines, so that it becomes impossible to reach the given degree of animal exhilaration unless there be, from time to time, an increase of the daily allowance.

3. To yield to this demand is certain ruin.

4. To fix a limit and maintain it involves of necessity, either a loss of the coveted enjoyment, or an endless, painful contest with an imperious appetite; and generally both.

Total abstinence then is the easiest position to defend in argument or maintain in practice, and the only position which is absolutely safe.

The needless use of so dangerous an agent is wrong. No man knows what perils he is preparing for himself when he places the cup at his lips. There may in his organization be dormant tendencies of which he has no suspicion. "Wine is a mocker." The habit makes its way by stealth. Even in its incipient stages it deludes with false impressions, and fills the mind with false counsels, so that the conscience fears no evil and utters no warning. It so distorts the vision that the careless navigator of this treacherous sea imagines that he is safe at anchor in calm and silent waters, where in reality a surf-beaten shore close at hand utters its hoarse murmurs and dashes its white foam, and a swift and resistless tide is drifting him steadily upon the fatal reef.

Men are indeed aware of the danger in general. They know it for each other, but not for themselves. Each sees the adder in his neighbor's cup, but finds nothing but joy in his own. Each knows that the spell is deepening upon his comrade. Each sees the gliding serpent noiselessly approaching his fellow victims, and throwing around them fold after fold; but he does not feel the cold and slimy coils which are winding and tightening about himself.

Let each look to his own safety. He who deems it a hardship utterly to renounce the insidious indulgence is not safe. He may not know his danger, but it is none the less real. Like one carelessly floating on the river above some tremendous cataract, he for a time glides smoothly along, past green isles whose shores are banks of violets, and whose sylvan bowers are vocal with the soft music of summer breezes and the songs of summer birds ; but soon walls of beetling rock shall be upon the right hand and the left, the hollow roar of the falling floods smite upon his ears, and the chafed current, every moment more swift, sweep him onward with resistless force, down to his doom.

CHAPTER XV.

ALCOHOL: THE STRENGTH OF THE ENEMY.

And when the servant of the man of God was risen early, and gone forth, behold, a host compassed the city both with horses and chariots. And his servant said unto him, Alas, my master! how shall we do?—2 KINGS.

IT becomes us to survey the field, and see what forces are in battle-array against us. It is never safe to under-estimate the power of the foe whom we are to encounter in deadly strife. In the present case, it is the height of folly for us to flatter ourselves with the hope of a brief combat and an easy victory. The enemy is strong in numbers, in pecuniary resources, in craft, and in that kind of courage which neither fears God nor regards man. It is intrenched in interest, prejudice and law, in custom, appetite and passion. A vast multitude incline to indulge in the perilous joy, and another host wish to make merchandise of the weakness of their fellow-men.

The first element of the strength of the enemy is found in the numbers given to indulgence.

The consumers of alcoholic beverages in the United States number millions. Many drink from the stress of a physical necessity which they themselves have created. They have incautiously indulged till the habit has mastered them. They are conscious that to change their course would involve so fierce a struggle with a despotic appetite that they have no courage to provoke the contest. They may cherish a vague hope of escape at some unknown future time, but they now lie passive in the grasp of the destroyer.

Many drink because they love the sensuous enjoyment, the present pleasure. They do not admit the existence of a habit, but they spend merry evenings among their comrades by the help of alcohol. To be sure, the mornings are apt to be dreary enough, but, as Lamb confesses, it seems to them an open question whether they will not lose by abstinence. They perceive no particular danger ahead; they confess no fear; they cannot be made to see any reason why they should give up their pleasures.

Many thoughtless men are forming the habit of using alcohol, not from any special love of it, or of the exhilaration which it usually produces, but because they are led by the love of the social enjoyment which they find in companies addicted to indulgence. The venders are cunning. They try to make their establishments as attractive as possible. They set their snares with ingenuity and nicest skill. They exert themselves to secure a nightly assemblage of jovial merry-makers, whose songs and stories will draw others, and hold the company together late, and thus help business.

It is not surprising that these establishments draw many into the trap. The man whose home is cheerless, the man who has no home, the youth who is away from his father's house, and has no comfortable, quiet place in which to spend his evenings, will be strongly tempted to enter the saloon, where he always finds a hearty welcome. And when fixed in these dangerous associations, but one result can follow. To enjoy the advantages of the house and spend nothing at the bar would be called mean. To keep such company and not fall into their ways would be unnatural. And soon a new fascination, a love of the animal exhilaration which alcohol creates, is added to the social attraction, and the prey is captured.

There are others, perhaps ranking high in the social scale, who really believe that they have it in their power to borrow temporary force of intellect from the drug, and are ready at any fancied emergency to have recourse to its treacherous promise of aid. A little sound truth, not altogether palatable, might break the snare in which these are caught. The seemingly augmented force borrowed of the narcotic is sheer delusion. The animal exhilaration which alcohol creates lulls their caution, and makes them bold to talk, and gives them a treacherous impression that they are outdoing themselves, when in fact they are belittled at every point, and the only real effect of the poison is to make them unconscious of their blunders.

Some drink deliberately for the purpose of drowning painful reflection. They have been unfortunate, or wicked, or both ; and they dread to be left alone with their own thoughts. Alcohol possesses the power to paralyze the intellect and fill the soul with an animal joy which, for the moment, sweeps away the sad memories of an ill-spent life. It is the natural resort of those who are unwilling to contemplate the past, and dare not face the present. Cowardice, meanness of spirit, prompts them to fly to premeditated delirium.

The demands of a certain style of fashionable life involve many in peril. He who aspires to live in "society," must make himself agreeable. He cannot associate with others on equal terms, unless he conform to usage. And so some set alcoholic beverages on their dinner tables, or provide them for the evening party, simply because they must do it, or find for themselves a new circle of acquaintances and friends.

A few fall into the habit because they are aiming at high life, and are under the impression that wine-bibbing is an indispensable part of it. They are generally those who have acquired wealth by their own exertions, perhaps in some questionable way, and are trusting to it to introduce them into regions, which, at an earlier period of their career, they were accustomed to stigmatize as aristocratic. Determined to be somebody, they set up a wine-cellar, just as they set up a carriage with a driver in livery, forgetting that these things no more make a true gentleman than a pair of epaulets constitute a true soldier. The compounder of wine regards these as his best customers, since they are chiefly anxious for high prices. And some drink occasionally without any visible motive. They seem to do it when they find the alcoholic beverage before them, just as they buy an apple or an orange when they happen to pass the places where fruit is vended.

Vicious methods of political engineering often lure victims into the power of the enemy. Unprincipled aspirants to office send their emissaries to the taverns and saloons, supplied with money to spend in ingratiating themselves with those who haunt such places, and gaining an influence over them which may be turned to account at the polls.

Thus the grand army of the consumers of alcohol is formed of many divisions, the rich and the poor, the high and the low, the wretches who rave in the drunkard's delirium or lie as dead men by the way-side, and those who carelessly sip their wine from time to time without a thought of the clouds which are gathering. It is a great host. It includes in the variegated ranks poverty and wealth, ignorance and learning, weakness and power, youth and age, some virtue and an infinity of vice and crime. It probably comprises a majority of the men and a few of the women of this nation.

To these we must add another force, another cohort of the powers of darkness, active, vigilant, unscrupulous and determined. These are the manufacturers and dealers. Their numbers are appalling. The records of the Department of Internal Revenue at Washington show that during the year ending June 30, 1869, taxes were paid by 5,333 wholesale dealers, and 121,910 retailers of intoxicating beverages. Add to these the clerks and bar keepers, and we have, at a very moderate estimate, a force of not less than 200,000 men. How many avoided payment we do not know. In the cities the number of drinking places is so great that the marvel is that they should all find support. In New York, for instance, Mr. Jourdan, the Superintendent of Police, acting under the instructions of the Board, caused a list of the names of the dealers, and their location, to be made in May, 1870; and his report shows that there were within the city limits at that date 6,359 places where spirituous or malt liquors, or both, were sold. This gives one liquor shop to 125 inhabitants. In 1869 the police authorities of Newark, N. J., made similar investigations, and ascertained that there were in that city 827 liquor dealers, or one to 130 inhabitants.

To this vast army whose sole business is to sell the drug, we must add the distillers, the brewers, and the "compounders of liquor," as the law delicately styles them; also the cultivators of hops, barley, and the other grains used—the thousands of men employed in various ways. Many are also involved in the business and share its unholy gains as owners of the buildings in which the manufacture or the sale is conducted. Making a reasonable estimate of these various classes and their families, we conclude that not fewer than one million of our people depend for a living upon the great national vice.

The drinking habits of the nation involve pecuniary interests of immense magnitude. Mr. Delano, the Commissioner of Internal Revenue, estimates the consumption of distilled spirits during the year 1869 at eighty millions of gallons. This quantity, rated merely as whisky, would be worth in the market eighty millions of dollars; if sold by the glass as whisky, it would cost the consumers at least five hundred millions of dollars.

Moreover, during the year ending June 30, 1869, the tax was paid on 5,790,746 barrels of fermented liquors manufactured. Sold by the glass, these beverages cost the consumer not less than one dollar a gallon, or one hundred and eighty millions of dollars for the whole quantity. There is no direct method by which the amount of the sales can be ascertained. Commissioner Wells, of the Department of Internal Revenue, estimated them in 1868 at six hundred millions annually. The American Year Book for 1869 estimates them at six hundred and forty-eight millions. As we have seen, if every barrel of fermented drinks pays the tax, and if the entire quantity of distilled liquors for which taxes were paid is retailed as rum or whisky, the gross amount of sales is six hundred and eighty millions of dollars annually. But this estimate does not cover the whole ground. On the one hand it does not allow for alcohol used for other purposes than as a beverage. On the other, it makes no allowance for importation, nor for illicit distilling, nor for fraudulent returns, nor for the increase of the quantity, and especially the increase of cost to the consumer, by innumerable frauds and adulterations. American wine-bibbers consume floods of liquids which are purchased by them as the pure, imported juice of the grape, but which are neither pure, nor imported, nor the juice of the grape. To prove this charge of fraud we have three distinct classes of facts.

The records of the Custom-House show that, in comparison with the immense amount of wine consumed, the quantity imported is ridiculously small. In 1850 the Hon. Mr. Kennedy, the Superintendent of the Census, stated in his report that the total imports of wine that year were valued at $2,370,000. The population of the United States at that time was 23,000,000. Consequently the importation amounted to just *ten cents' worth* of foreign wine for each inhabitant. In 1869, the wine imported was only sufficient to give each of our people *six cents' worth.* The foreign brandy imported the same year sufficed to furnish each of our people with less than two cents' worth. Foreign countries, therefore, supply us with a sufficient amount of wine and brandy to give each of our people about eight cents' worth annually; and all over this quantity is concocted here at home.

Again, it is well known that liquor dealers have long had in their possession, and in use, recipes which they have tried to keep a secret from the consumers, and which give directions how to make cheap imitations of various alcoholic beverages. The materials named are cider, whisky, rum, and sundry poisons of the most virulent character. One recipe lying before me tells me how to make "Port wine" without a particle of the juice of the grape; another tells us how to make a "fine old brandy" in twelve days.

We have also the testimony of the civil courts. For instance, in May, 1866, a case of alleged smuggling was tried at Albany, N. Y., in the U. S. District Court. The article in dispute consisted of several casks of what seemed to be foreign brandy, which had not paid the duty. The District Attorney called as witnesses a druggist and an experienced hotel keeper, who, after tasting, pronounced it genuine French brandy, such as they were accustomed to pay for at the rate of twelve and fifteen dollars a gallon. The defense proved conclusively that the liquor, and even the cask which contained it, were only skillful imitations of the genuine article. One extensive dealer testified that he had not sold one gallon of French brandy in ten years; that the drugged mixtures for imitating it are regularly manufactured and sold; and that very little genuine liquor of any kind is known in this country. But with the records of the Custom-House to show that the wine and brandy imported supply only eight cents' worth annually for each of our people, it requires no additional evidence to demonstrate the existence of gigantic frauds in the liquor trade.

Moreover, the enemy has not only numbers and wealth, but organization. Through the length and breadth of the land the dealers are banded together, and make common cause in defence of their unholy gains. Funds are collected to influence elections, to resist the arm of the law, to prevent restrictive legislation, or render it inoperative. Whatever craft, audacity, and unscrupulous determination can do to defeat the efforts of the friends of temperance will be done. Look, then, at the strength of the enemy. A large majority of our people are either drifting along carelessly on the outer circles of the whirlpool, or are already swept along by a tide which they cannot resist. One million of our population are supported by the traffic, and all their interests are involved in maintaining and extending it. The laws of nearly all the States in the Union give it a strong moral support under color of regulating it. Politicians, editors, and parties, elections and legislation, are bought and sold by it. Appetite and avarice, fashion, prejudice, and law, defend it. Every villainy in the land is ready to stand up in its defense, and every element of human depravity rallies to its support.

CHAPTER XVI.

ALCOHOL: THE DAMAGE DONE.

And when I looked, behold, a hand was sent unto me; and lo, a roll of a book was therein; and he spread it before me; and it was written within and without: and there was written therein lamentations, and mourning, and woe.—EZEKIEL.

WHO shall estimate the extent of the ruin wrought? When we reflect that the actual cost of alcoholic beverages, as paid by consumers, cannot be less than six hundred and eighty millions of dollars annually; that an army of at least two hundred thousand men are engaged in the sale, and that the consumers of all grades number millions, we can anticipate only evil results on a scale corresponding with the magnitude of the agencies at work.

THE WASTE.

The first prominent fact brought to light in the investigation is the enormous waste of the elements of material prosperity. The entire amount paid for intoxicating drinks must be set down as absolutely lost.

It is urged, indeed, that, according to our own estimates, the manufacture and sale furnish employment and support for one million of our people, and therefore form an important and valuable branch of our industrial interests. It is also urged that the money spent in the dram-shop is paid out again, reaching in turn the wholesale dealer, the manufacturer, the workman, the farmer, and all the rest of the long series, and therefore there is no loss, but a positive gain.

This is utter delusion. The Government of the United States collects annually one hundred and twenty millions of dollars to pay the interest of the national debt, and the money thus collected all goes back again among the people. Is the national debt therefore no burden? The money collected by law for the support of the poor is all paid out again for food, clothing, and supplies of various kinds. Are taxes, therefore, to be accounted a financial blessing? And if the fact that so many people derive their support from the manufacture and sale is proof that the traffic is a valuable public interest, what shall we say of picking pockets? Do not men and women get their living and support their families in this way? Do not thieves and gamblers keep money in circulation? If the reasoning holds good in the case of alcohol, it is equally valid in regard to the thousand evil devices whereby wicked and lazy people try to get a living without earning it.

The fallacy of the arguments offered in defense of the alcoholic interest is so transparent that it is doubtful whether any amount of explanation will make it clearer. Money merely aids in the exchange of commodities. It enables the farmer or the mechanic to trade the things which he produces for others which he needs. The farmer raises wheat, and by means of money exchanges it for cloth, sugar, nails, a new carriage or a new house. The shoemaker, by means of bank bills, sells his shoes for wheat and beef. The bank bills themselves get their sole value from the fact that they can be used to buy what we want. They only enable us to trade what we do not need for that which we wish to obtain.

The test of utility is to inquire what each man is doing for others in return for what he receives from them. The farmer furnishes wheat and beef, and receives cloth, shoes, and hats. The weaver furnishes cloth, and receives wheat, and beef, shoes and hats. The shoemaker and the hatter supply their useful products, and in exchange receive the products of others. The vender of alcohol receives wheat and beef; his wants are supplied by the labors of others; but what does he give in return? Nothing. He rewards those who support him by poisoning them. If his wares were harmless as well as worthless, he would be only a pauper. As the case stands, he is a public enemy.

What is added to the common good by the grand army of some 200,000 men whose sole business is to mix drink for the nation? What is added to the public well-being by the 56,663 men, who, according to the "Brewers' Congress" of 1869, are employed, directly or indirectly, in supplying the American people with beer? Unless it can be shown that the intoxicants consumed make a real addition to human comfort and rational enjoyment, and promote the true welfare of men, the business is doing no true service. But there is not an honest man in America who will say that this alcoholic deluge is a public good. Every intelligent man knows that the millions of money thus spent are as utterly lost as if sunk in the sea, and that the crowds of men who live by the manufacture and sale of alcoholic drinks are a worse public burden than so many paupers. They are hungry leeches, draining the nation's blood; they are the maggots which breed in its festering wounds.

The magnitude of the pecuniary loss will be better seen when we compare it with the aggregate of the national possessions. The census of 1850 shows that the real estate and the personal property of the American people were assessed that year at $6,009,000,000, which represents all that the nation had accumulated by two centuries and a half of toil. But the present annual outlay for intoxicating beverages is $680,000,000. It follows, then, that if the American people continue to drink at the present rate, they will sink in this bottomless gulf, within the next ten years, a sum of money equal to the assessed value of all that the nation possessed in 1850, its lands, its houses, its mines, its slaves, its shipping, its property of every description, the accumulations of two hundred and fifty years.

In 1860 the assessed value of the national wealth was $12,084,000,000. The gain for the ten years was therefore $6,075,000,000 or $607,000,000 a year. This gain includes the value of new lands brought into cultivation, the improvements made in all the national domain, the rise in the value of real estate every-where, and the increase of personal property of all kinds. The present annual outlay for intoxicants, therefore, equals the annual addition to the national wealth during the ten years ending in 1860, a period during which eight millions were added to the population.

To give it another form, this nation is thus squandering each year a sum equal to the entire valuation of the four sovereign states of California, Iowa, Maine and Kansas in 1860.*

To put it in still another shape, the entire earnings of the nation in 1869, according to the estimates of Commissioner Wells, amounted to $6,285,000,000. Consequently, of this vast

* Valuation of	California........	$207,874,613
"	Iowa............	247,338,265
"	Maine...........	190,211,600
"	Kansas..........	31,327,895
		$676,752 373

Report of Eighth Census, p. 195.

sum, the fruit of the industry of forty millions of people, their farms, factories, mines, railroads, etc., every tenth dollar is swept into the till of the liquor vender.

The magnitude of the loss will justify another illustration. Mr. Wells estimates the national wealth in 1870, at $23,400,000,000. This gives an average of $600 for each inhabitant. Consequently, alcohol costs the nation every year a sum equal to the entire possessions of one million of our people.

But to the actual cost of the liquors consumed, we must add the waste of time, the detriment done in every way to the industry of the nation, whereby the earnings of every branch of labor are lessened, and the substance of the people is wasted. Add to the direct outlay for intoxicants, the cost of the idleness, the crime, and the pauperism caused by alcohol, and the total loss and damage would probably reach eight hundred, or even a thousand millions of dollars. We are certainly within bounds when we conclude that if we were free from all the losses and waste which the drinking habits of our people produce, the wealth of the nation would increase at twice the present rate.

CRIME.

When we consider the tendency of alcohol to darken the reason, deaden the moral sensibilities, and set the passions free from control, we infer at once that the common use of so debasing an intoxicant must increase offenses against the laws. All experience justifies the inference. Indeed, if the deliberate statements of magistrates, and the wardens and chaplains of prisons are reliable, alcohol is the chief cause of crime.

The Rev. J. B. Finley, some years ago chaplain of the Ohio State Penitentiary, describes the case of a prisoner sentenced for homicide, and adds:

"But the man who sold the whisky is the great sinner, after all. He was the procuring cause of the crime for which this man suffers. The same is true of nine-tenths of all the crime committed in the country."--*Memorials of Prison Life*, p. 163.

The Rev. Louis Dwight, Secretary of the American Prison Discipline Society, says: "Four fifths of all the inmates committed their crimes under the influence of these liquors."

The Board of State Charities of Massachusetts, in their Report to the Legislature in 1868, say:

"The prison registers indicate that more than two thirds of the criminals in the State are the victims of intemperance; but the proportion of crime traceable to this great vice must be set down at not less than four fifths."

The warden of a prison in the same State makes the following statement:

"Since I have been connected with the prison we have had twenty-one convicts here for killing their wives, two for killing their fathers, and one for killing his mother. Of these twenty-four, all but one were not only habitual drunkards, but were actually drunk when they committed the crime."

Nor is the experience of other nations unlike our own. The Hon. Mr. Buxton, of London, declares that "it is intoxication that fills our jails." Rowland Burr, Esq., for nearly twenty years a magistrate at Toronto, stated to the Canadian Parliament that nine tenths of the male prisoners, and nineteen twentieths of the female, are sent to jail by intoxicating liquors. Judge Patteson, at the Assizes at Norwich, England, said to the Grand Jury, "If it were not for this drinking, you and I would have nothing to do."

But why multiply quotations? The facts have been set forth again and again. They stand unimpeached and unimpeachable. It is proved before the world that alcohol is a most prolific cause of crime.

PAUPERISM.

In this favored land, where a vast breadth of fertile soil, as yet unbroken by the plow, invites labor and promises food for uncounted millions, abject poverty ought to be unknown, save in the case of those misfortunes which fall alike upon "the evil and the good, the just and the unjust." Yet in the year 1850 the national statistics, which are the latest I have been able to obtain, show that there was one pauper to one hundred and seventy-two of the entire population of the country. Poverty exists in various localities in proportion to the number of grog-shops. In New York city, as we have seen, there is a retailer of alcohol for every one hundred and twenty-five people. The official reports of 1860 show that one native American and three foreigners out of every twenty-five of the entire population received relief from the public authorities that year.

The condition of older countries shows still more fearful ravages. In England, in 1859, one in twenty-two of the whole population was supported wholly or in part from the poor funds. France, in 1853, expended twenty millions of dollars for the poor. In Holland, in 1855, where one town alone contains one hundred and seventy-two distilleries for the manufacture of gin, one in twelve of the people was a pauper. In Belgium the pauperism is still greater.

Nor are we convinced that the crowded state of European populations alone causes the evil. This certainly aggravates it; nevertheless, we have the most convincing evidence to show that it is not so much the lack of employment as it is the habits of the people that overwhelms them in want. England spends annually five hundred millions of dollars for beer and spirits; and the greater part of this enormous sum comes from the very classes which supply the hosts of paupers. The Hon. Charles Buxton, whom we have already quoted in another place, says in regard to the English poor: "It is intoxication that fills our work-houses with poor. Were it not for this one cause, pauperism would be nearly extinguished in England."

This view of the case is supported by the Westminster Review, which says:

"Drunkenness is the curse of England, a curse so great that it far eclipses every other calamity. It is impossible to exaggerate the evils of drunkenness."

The same fearful agency is at work in America; and the effects which already appear are sufficient to create alarm. Already an army of probably three hundred thousand paupers is supported by public charity; and patient and impartial investigation has shown that about two thirds of them are brought to want directly or indirectly by alcohol. Here is misery enough, without our waiting for worse results.

INSANITY.

Knowing how alcohol expends its force chiefly upon the brain, we would naturally infer that, where the use of it becomes a habit, there is danger of such disease as affects the mind itself. We have evidence of the most conclusive description in regard to the actual result.

Dr. Carpenter of London, one of the highest authorities in his profession, says:

"We have no difficulty in understanding how the habitual use of alcoholic liquors in excess becomes one of the most frequent causes of insanity. Upon this point all writers on the subject are agreed."—"*Physiology*," *etc.*, p. 34.

Dr. Hiram Cox, of Cincinnati, Ohio, whose official duty for years was to examine cases of alleged mental disease, states that two thirds of the insane persons who thus came under his notice, were made such by alcohol.

Lord Shaftesbury, at a public address at Manchester not long since, said: "Here I speak of my own knowledge and experience, having acted as a Commissioner of Lunacy for the last twenty years. Fully six out of ten of all cases of insanity arise from no other cause than from habits of intemperance."

Mr. Kennedy, the Superintendent of the Census of 1860, says that intemperance is probably the most productive of all the causes of insanity in America.

But why pursue these sad details further? The drinking habits of our people lessen every element of individual and national well-being, and assail every public and private interest. They multiply every public burden; they render the persons and the property of good citizens less safe; they lure youth to its ruin; they despoil manhood of its strength; they fill old age with sorrow. They are the great obstacle in the way of national progress, the active and relentless enemy of peace, virtue and happiness.

What the final result will be among the nations given to alcohol, no man can tell. While the Persians retained their simple habits, and, as Herodotus informs us, "drank water only," they were conquerors. Sparta, Athens and Macedon were powerful till luxury overcame them. For six hundred years after the building of Rome, the vine was not cultivated, and her legions were invincible. But Babylon and Greece and Rome fell by wealth and effeminacy. Vice lost that which virtue had won. Drunkenness destroyed the power which sobriety had created.

How far popular education, the press, and a truer religion will enable modern nations to resist decay remains to be seen. We are told by the English historian, Mr. Froude, that the best days of the British Empire are past, and that England is on the decline. Every lover of human progress will be slow to believe this; but of one fact there can be no doubt, the heaviest millstone that drags her down is the drinking habits of her people. Intemperance is the rending devil under whose malignant power she "wallows foaming."

We are more nearly allied to England than to any other nation, by blood, religion and literature, and we tend to follow in her footsteps. The drinking habits of our people cast by far the gloomiest shadow that rests upon our national path.

CHAPTER XVII.

ALCOHOL: REMEDIAL MEASURES.

Who is on the Lord's side?—EXODUS.

HOW long must this tremendous evil be the scourge of even Christian communities? How shall the nations be rescued from the strangling coils of the gigantic serpent which is crushing out their life?

We have no right to cease working. The friends of reform have seen their labors crowned with successes which are enough to fill every humane heart with joy; victories which, we trust, are only the harbingers of complete and universal triumph. Let us glance at some of them, that we may gain from the contemplation new courage for the weary warfare. Science has thoroughly examined the properties of alcohol, and pronounced it essentially a poison. The medical profession has spoken, declaring the common use of alcohol by men in health both useless and dangerous. Political economists confess that the popular use of intoxicants is detrimental to the State, an ulcer in the body politic, an evil which assumes such dimensions as make the legal management of it the great legislative problem of the day. Religious bodies are ranging themselves more and more decidedly in favor of entire abstinence, in theory and practice.

The accursed liquor traffic, too, is sinking lower in public estimation every day, and a darker stigma is fixed upon those engaged in the murderous work. It has become evident to every American patriot that the drinking habits of our people are the sin, the shame, the burden of the nation ; and that from this quarter comes up the blackest cloud that hangs over the historic future. Public opinion on the general subject has changed marvelously within the last fifty years, and the progress still continues.

Whole classes of the community have been brought from darkness to light, and from imminent peril to comparative safety. The debate is ended, and the temperance argument is triumphant. The reform gathers its forces for aggressive action. The best and most intelligent portions of our people, alarmed at the magnitude of the vice, are preparing for a desperate contest with it.

The reform, indeed, wins its way slowly, and perhaps will continue so to move for years to come. Great reforms move slowly because they involve great interests, and are opposed by great forces. They therefore demand corresponding conviction, faith and courage.

The *doctrines* of the reform are determined. No friend of temperance now expects to win the victory under any other banner than that of Total Abstinence.

That there is danger in the attempt to use distilled liquors in moderation, needs no proof. Even in small doses the drug asserts its peculiar power. The whole system becomes enslaved by the narcotic, and when temporarily deprived of it, is morbidly restless and out of tune; to secure the coveted animal exhilaration requires a continual increase of the quantity, and the hold of the intoxicant upon the victim strengthens with every addition.

Nor can milder intoxicants be used with advantage as a substitute for worse. When lager beer was introduced here, its advocates confidently argued that it would take the place of stronger inebriants, and thus promote sobriety. What is the fact? The beer saloon is doing even more injury than the tavern. It is not so public a place of resort. A screen at the door and curtains at the windows shut in the victim. There the band of doomed ones gathers night after night. Young men are lured into the secret den, who dare not be seen lounging at the hotel; and often before their friends suspect that any thing is wrong they are ruined.

And men can be intoxicated with beer as well

as with brandy. Beer does the work with equal certainty, and the effects are equally debasing. Every intelligent reader of the daily journals will bear witness that more brawls and bloodshed, more cases of violence by shooting, stabbing and otherwise, originate in the beer saloons than in all other places of public resort.

The experience of other countries agrees with our own. English statesmen imagined in 1830 that, by licensing beer shops, the consumption of spirits would decrease, and thus the nation would be rescued from the accumulating horrors of intemperance. The plan is folly in theory and a failure in practice. So deplorable have been the effects of the measure that Lord Brougham, who had been sanguine of good results, moved the repeal of the law. The repeal has not yet been effected, but public opinion is steadily accumulating against the law, and its abrogation cannot be much longer deferred. One of the most significant signs of the times in England is the recent action of the leading clergy of the established Church. The Convocation of Canterbury appointed a large committee of the ablest ministers to examine the general subject; and in their long and interesting report, among other measures proposed to arrest the tide of evil, the committee urge "the total suppression of beer houses throughout the country." Total abstinence, then, is felt to be the only solid basis of reformatory action.

We inquire, next, what are the *active forces* of reform?

Among these forces the *Christian Church* must ever stand foremost. For the world to fight this great beneficent battle, while the Church looked on timidly from afar, would be a deep and lasting disgrace to all that bear the Christian name. While it repels no sincere adherent, nor refuses a place to any honest worker, the reform must ally itself to the religious convictions of the people. Nor can the general community be urged one hair-breadth beyond the position occupied by the Churches.

As the Church goes forward, the community may advance with it; but they will never go beyond it.

The position which the Churches are in duty bound to take is not hard to be seen. They should be wholly free from the sin of indulgence in alcohol. The Church should steadily refuse to share the unholy gains of the cruel traffic. It must not suffer unworthy members of its communion to sell its good name for the base bribes of the iniquitous business, and, while they are guilty of this treachery, wink at their conduct because of their liberal donations for Church purposes.

And the ministry must neither be silent nor give an uncertain sound. The pulpit is divinely ordained to deal with the dangers of the hour, and the sins of the people. If, through a timid or mercenary policy, it fails of its high duty, then it ceases to speak for God; it becomes a mere secular agency conducted for the emolument of the time-serving incumbent, or to secure the worldly purposes of those who keep it in bondage. The blood of the slain will cling to the watchman who saw the sword coming, but who meanly cared for nothing but his own ease, and was dumb. The curse of the Master will rest upon the membership who bore his name while they banded together to prevent his truth from being spoken.

But the American clergy, considered as a body, are the leaders of this great reform. O that they would speak out yet more boldly! O that they were armed with mightier faith and new courage for the battle! And while I am glad to know that what has been done has been accomplished chiefly by Christian hands, I cannot forbear to put on record my profound conviction, that until there are in the Churches, both in England and America, a deeper sense of duty, and a firmer courage and a more active energy in doing it, the day of final victory will not dawn.

We feel that the Utah abomination is the

shame of our civilization; that the erection of heathen temples in California is a reproach to our religion. But a dram-shop in Boston or Philadelphia is a greater reproach to us than is a Chinese Joss-house in San Francisco, or polygamy at Salt Lake. The heathen worship is an importation, an alien. The Utah iniquity flies into the desert, and by flight alone prolongs its hateful existence. But the liquor shop, the most murderous piece of Satanic enginery in operation among us, the prolific source of crime, poverty and wretchedness of every description, stands under the very shadow of the Church, and stands strong, too often, because it is upheld by the very hands which in Church assemblies are held up in hypocritic prayer, and because the pulpit is either silent in regard to the foul wrong, or feebly cries Peace, peace, where God and humanity demand relentless war.

Lectures.—Too many lecturers of the right kind cannot be set to work; and every efficient worker is entitled to fair compensation for his labor. Still, care must be taken to prevent unworthy men from making merchandise of a good cause. This was the bane of the Washingtonian movement. Let no one be employed, or in any way countenanced, unless his chief aim is to gain adherents to right principles. We want men to urge this reform, who are as earnest in the work as ever John the Baptist was in preaching repentance, and who have as little fear of Herod. The community need not mere amusement, but the deep, thorough, pungent conviction which secures earnest, resolute action. The argument of this reform must be pressed upon public attention in all available ways, until it is securely lodged in the public mind and conscience. Temperance meetings and temperance lectures, of the right kind, cannot be multiplied beyond the popular need.

Organizations.—The Good Templars, with their 360,000 members, the Sons of Temperance with 100,000, and the Temple of Honor with 20,000, are doing a noble work. They deserve the favor of good men every-where. They are not "Secret Societies" in any objectionable sense of the terms. They avow their principles and their aims; their members are known; their methods of working are no secret. They have done and are still doing efficient service, and there are fields into which none can enter so well as they. It ought also to be said in their praise that, in times of general apathy, when others seemed ready to lay down the weapons of their warfare and leave the enemy to go on with his evil work unmolested, these organizations, undismayed and unconquerable, have kept an active force in the field, and confronted the foe with their solid strength.

The General Society should not be suffered to fall into decay. We need in every ward of the cities and in every country neighborhood a society which all the people, old and young, may be invited to join, the sole condition of membership being the signing and the keeping of the pledge. Frequent public meetings should be held, and the pledge be offered for signature at every meeting. The members of the divisions and lodges of the various temperance orders should engage heartily in this work. They will thus greatly promote the stability and growth of their own organizations.

The Press is an indispensable agent of the reform. We must have books and periodicals in abundance, and those, too, which will make their way every-where, secure attention and compel conviction. We need a publishing house ably officered, and abundant in resources, equal to those of the various Christian denominations. We have indeed made a beginning. The Publication House established in New York by the National Temperance Society does honor to the liberality and zeal of its founders. It is already a power in the land. Still, compared with the work to be done, this publishing agency is lamentably deficient in resources. Its entire capital is no more than the liquor interest often spends in defending a single case of illegal sale; it is not a tenth part of the sum which the venders often pay in the attempt to influence a legislature. We require, in fact, a publication office with a building, appliances, and income like the American Bible Society, and, like it, able to place its books and periodicals in every house in all the land. Even then our means would hardly equal our wants. Look at the strength of the liquor interest. Its income is at least six hundred and eighty millions of dollars a year. It is the sole business of two hundred thousand men to pour out the alcoholic venom. One million of our people live by means of this tide of death. Will this compact force, organized, active, alert, determined, bound together by every avaricious incentive and selfish principle, be overcome by skirmishing and border raids? Alas! we have been battering Gibraltar with snow-balls. Until patriotism, humanity, and religion prompt to more vigorous measures, the reform will drag its slow length along, the derision of its enemies and the grief of its friends. Instead of sending forth a fleet strong enough to sweep the cruel pirates from the sea, we are working with a little life-boat, glad when we are able to pick up a wounded man thrown overboard from a burning ship, or to give decent burial to the corpse of some poor victim.

Personal Effort must not be undervalued nor neglected. Let every one who loves the right stand up in its defense. Moral influence is powerful. If every man and woman who is convinced of the need of this reform should make it a point to say calmly every day, in the presence of at least one person, "I believe that the common use of alcoholic drinks is useless, dangerous, and wrong," would it be breath spent in vain? I believe that there is an amount of conviction lying silent in the minds of men sufficient to achieve a great work if it could have bold and persistent utterance. Let each begin just where he stands, the mother talking with her children, friend with friend, the employer with his workmen, the merchant with his clerks, neighbor with neighbor, the traveler with the stranger. Not only by the set address and the elaborate volume, but by the casual word and the brief and thoughtful remark, do reforms progress and the right conquer.

In a word, the whole list of our remedial measures may be set forth in one brief phrase, Work, and the means with which to work. We need men, money, organization, faith, hope, an energy that never flags, and a courage that never flinches. There is no new way of easy victory. There is no subtle device, no ingenious strategy, by which we may turn this mighty struggle into a pleasant pastime. It is stern, relentless war. It will cost money, and toil, and anxiety, and tears, and possibly blood. As the reform progresses, the less hardened venders and manufacturers will give way before the force of advancing public sentiment, and worse men will take their places. The last cohort to be routed will be composed of reckless, desperate men, impervious to shame, men of the same moral grade as the professional thieves and burglars by whom our cities are infested, fit subjects only for the iron hand of the law.

And to this complexion we come at last. Law, based on the same settled public conviction which now demands that theft, riot, and murder shall be suppressed, must suppress the liquor traffic. Society has a right to protect itself against a public enemy. The manufacture and sale of alcohol as a means of indulgence are immoral. The business is essentially dishonest, treacherous, and cruel; a thing to be despised, abhorred, and hated; and no civil government that does not aim to suppress it has risen to a true conception of its high office.

In fine, we stand face to face with a gigantic antagonist who is remorseless in his purpose and unscrupulous in regard to means, and who will resist unto death. There is no place for diplomacy or strategy. Fighting hand to hand, foot to foot, with this powerful foe, we must contend for the nation's life, and suffer defeat, or gain at the best a hard won victory. And the saddest thought of all is that there should be among those who ought to be foremost in the action so much reluctance to act, so much apathy in regard to the ruin wrought before their very eyes. We are like the dwellers in a lofty mansion built on some dangerous coast where frequent wrecks occur. Darkness and storm may be without, but we are safe, and full of peace and comfort within. A ship crowded with passengers is going to pieces among the rocks and we know it. We see the red flash of the alarm-guns, and hear the booming signal that death is at work and help is needed. But we are safe. We look around at the circle of loved ones; we glance at the cheerful fire, the table, the books, the pictured walls. Yes, we are safe. Faintly amid the roar of the winds and the sea we hear imploring voices, but we are safe. We sing our evening song of praise, we say our evening prayer. We retire to our beds and fall asleep to the sound of storm and surf, and imploring voices still more faintly heard, while all through the night, one after another, men, women, and little innocent children are dropping, dropping from the icy wreck, and the busy waves are piling the dead along the shore under our very windows.

NOTICES OF THE PRESS.

We have at last something new and original in the literature of the temperance cause. The treatise is a learned one; but the style is spirited and simple, and so plain that a child may understand it. . . . Happy is that man who can bring to a moral enterprise the re-inforcement of fresh and vigorous ideas. This benediction must rest upon the head of our friend, Dr. J. T. Crane. He comes to the front of the temperance ranks, and offers valuable service at an hour when his new weapon is peculiarly adapted to the result sought. It is a fresh and original form of presenting an old and worn theme, and has been so successfully executed that it will force a hearing from those who, through familiarity with the topic, have ceased to be interested in it. The style is so lively and clear, and the volume is so full of entertaining as well as startling information, that our young people will be sure to read it if it is once placed in their hands.—*Christian Advocate.*

The appearance of this neat and timely volume will be hailed with great satisfaction by the friends of humanity. The question of intoxicants is discussed with a broader range than usual.—*Methodist.*

"*The Arts of Intoxication.*"—Dr. Crane has grappled with a mighty subject, and done it grandly. He gives the history in outline of intoxication in ancient and modern times, and deals with the varied aspects of his theme as a philosopher, a philanthropist, and a Christian. He has crowded an immense amount of valuable information into the compass of a beautiful little volume. It is a work of decided merit. We commend it to all our readers, old and young, ministers and laymen. The facts and figures may seem astounding, but no charge of exaggeration will be sustained against the author.—*Western Christian Advocate.*

Dr. Crane has placed the community under obligations for a volume of rare excellence, as a treatise upon all the means of intoxication and their effects. It is valuable as a text-book upon a subject of vital importance.—*New Jersey Journal.*

We earnestly recommend it as a strong plea in behalf of temperance, and one which should be liberally circulated and read by members of temperance organizations, as supplying abundant arguments against the use and abuse of the bane of civilization.—*Sussex Register.*

We have read it from preface to conclusion with constantly increasing interest. The book is characterized by great breadth and range of thought, by fairness and thoroughness of argument, and by an unusual amount of practical common sense. It is a work of no ordinary merit; the most valuable contribution to temperance literature that has appeared for a long time.—*Orange Journal.*

The results of the most careful scientific research are carefully stated, while the moral and religious conclusions are presented with great earnestness and power. The book is valuable, timely, thorough, and suggestive.—*Newark Courier.*

Written in a very captivating style, that attracts and holds the reader's attention to the close.—*Newark Journal.*

We consider this little volume a valuable addition to temperance literature, and worthy of a place in the library of every family. We most cheerfully commend it to the active advocates of the temperance reform as a most thorough discussion of the subject, and one which will greatly aid them in their work.—STEPHEN B. RANSOM, *Most Worthy Patriarch of the National Division of the Sons of Temperance.*

It is just the work needed at the present time, and it should have a large circulation. Dr. Crane's style is very attractive, rising at times to true eloquence. We commend it to all interested in the cause.—*Boston Nation.*

No addition to the literature of the temperance reform, so able, conclusive, and impressive as this, has been made for a long time. The work will at once take its high place as an argument and plea, as a weapon of offense and a shield, and be among the foremost standard-bearers in the good cause. The evident research, the candor, the perspicuity, the scientific care, and the religious spirit that mark the work, make it peculiarly fitted to reach a class of minds that have hitherto withstood arguments and statements not so deftly or decorously presented. Let the work have wide circulation.—*S. S. Times* (Philadelphia.)

Dr. Crane is an animated and forcible writer, and he has condensed the temperance argument within the compass of a small duodecimo in a very skillful and interesting manner. He is absolutely uncompromising, however, upon the subject of the use of stimulants. . . . It will be admitted by all who read this little volume that Dr. Crane is an earnest and eloquent advocate of total abstinence. We might even say that as an essayist he is the peer of Gough as a lecturer.—*New York Evening Post.*

Of all the books written in the interest of temperance, we think of none better adapted to be generally useful. It gives a great deal of valuable information, drawn from a wide circle of reading. It is an able plea and argument, and a valuable contribution to the science and conduct of life.—*Newark Daily Advertiser.*

Dr. Crane on Popular Amusements.

16mo., pp. 209. Price, $1.

THE SECOND EDITION OF THIS NEW WORK IS PUBLISHED.

OPINIONS OF THE PRESS.

We doubt if the line can be more wisely drawn. Dr. Crane's work is done in his best style. There are logic, rhetoric, philosophy, and now and then some lively "amusement" in it.—*Methodist Quarterly Review.*

In this volume there is a happy medium between a sour asceticism and free license of worldliness. We trust its wide circulation will prove that it is duly appreciated.—*Christian Advocate.*

We commend this volume to the perusal of our ministers, and then urge them to see its free circulation among their people.—*Ladies' Repository.*

It is a timely production, and will do much to combat mischievous popular amusements, as well as to introduce a harmless and beneficial class of recreations.—*Methodist.*

Dr. Crane takes the only tenable ground respecting the amusements most generally practiced among fashionable society. Its cautions should be duly heeded.—*Good News.*

It is a capital work: we wish it were in every family. Readers will find it written in an entertaining style, and we are very sure they cannot escape from the grip of its logic. We advise Pastors and leaders to send for it.—*Nashville Christian Advocate.*

No more timely or valuable book has issued from the Methodist press in a long time. The author is a writer of rare ability and graceful style. Pastors can do no better service in their charges than to scatter it all around them.—*Western Christian Advocate.*

www.ingramcontent.com/pod-product-compliance
Lightning Source LLC
LaVergne TN
LVHW010237110826
845151LV00004B/1320

* 9 7 8 1 4 2 5 5 2 3 9 8 5 *